Travel While You Work:
The Ultimate Guide To Running A Business From Anywhere

Mish Slade

Copyright © Mish Slade 2015

All rights reserved. This book is sold subject to the condition that it shall not, by way of trade or otherwise, be lent, re-sold, hired out or otherwise circulated in any form of binding or cover other than that in which it is published and without a similar condition including this condition being imposed on the subsequent purchaser.

Contents

BEFORE YOU GET STARTED...

Introduction 1

What does this lifestyle look like? 5

Which chapters should you read? 9

SECTION 1: SETTLING IN, LOGISTICS AND SAFETY

Chapter 1: Settle In Fast 15

Chapter 2: Get To Grips With Money And Taxes 51

Chapter 3: Guard Your Data 73

SECTION 2: GETTING DOWN TO BUSINESS

Chapter 4: Be A Productivity Powerhouse 85

Chapter 5: Freelance From Anywhere 105

Chapter 6: Hire Like A Champ 129

Chapter 7: Run The Best Biz 167

Bonus Chapter: Travel Like A Pro 191

Conclusion 213

APPENDIX: INTERVIEWS

Part 1: Different types of digital nomad 217

Part 2: Advice from families who travel 311

RESOURCES

List of links 331

Introduction

When my husband Rob and I first became "digital nomads" back in 2012, the term barely existed. And whenever it *was* used, it sounded pretentious and tacky. (Admittedly it still sounds that way, but no one has yet come up with a suitable replacement shorthand for "someone whose work doesn't require them to be in a particular place and can be done largely online".) It also sounded like a passing phase – something for a few wannabe free spirits to try out before realising that the lifestyle is unsustainable in the long term.

A mere three years later and – while the term itself isn't ubiquitous as such – it's becoming more and more widely understood that travelling while you work is not only *totally* possible but also extremely fulfilling.

I'm not just talking about freelance web designers, programmers, writers and travel bloggers; I'm talking about accountants, lawyers, therapists and teachers. Fitness trainers, economists, photographers and business consultants. Not to mention entire businesses that have chosen to do away with a centralised office, and instead hire and manage a distributed team who live around the world.

So why do they (and we) do it?

Essentially, it's about freedom. As you'll discover when you read this book, being a digital nomad affords you the type of flexibility and autonomy that you couldn't enjoy as an employee or business owner working out of an office. And that freedom extends much further than just "the ability to travel a lot". Yes: you'll have set up a life and business in such a way that enables you to experience the world at your own pace, rather than squeezed into an annual two-week vacation. But you'll also grant yourself the ability to do away with (or at least question) everything that's taken for granted in regular working environments.

You don't have to work 9-to-5 if those aren't your most productive hours, for example. You don't have to commute. If you're a business owner, you can hire staff from anywhere around the world – rather than from the far smaller selection of people who live near "the office" or would be willing to travel there. If you're a freelancer, you can – at a moment's notice – decide not to take on so many clients for a few months (just because) and move to Thailand to save money.

Being a digital nomad is possible and doable for the majority of professions – just head to the Appendix for some interviews and inspiration. But it demands a certain set of skills and know-how in order to be enjoyable and productive. This is especially true if you're planning to set up a business and manage a team on the move, but it's still the case if you simply want to freelance or become a remote worker for someone else's company.

And that's where I come in. To help, that is. I started out as a freelancing digital nomad (doing copywriting and web project management under the company name "Mortified Cow"), and later – while continuing with the freelancing – worked with Rob to set up our own business.

The business is called Yellow Lettings; it helps landlords to find tenants for their rental properties, and then manages the entire lettings process (rent collection, inspections, maintenance, legalities and a whole lot more) for them.

We came up with the name in Barcelona, set up the basic structure of the business in Thailand, conducted interviews for our first hire in Edinburgh, and launched the website from Prague. Meanwhile, our co-founder is in London, our first seven employees are all in different cities around the UK, and we routinely hire contractors who live anywhere from Sri Lanka to Bulgaria.

And between this remote business and our freelancing experience, we've learnt *a lot* about what it takes to travel while working. We know how to get settled into a new city in super-quick time. We've discovered the best methods for hiring contractors and permanent members of staff without needing to interview them in person. We've figured out (after an incredible amount of trial and error) how to manage and communicate with our team of staff and contractors around the world. We know the best methods for dealing with clients as a freelancer. We've found out about some nifty tools for receiving cross-currency payments without losing a ton of cash to conversion fees. And we've developed some mindset hacks for maintaining our productivity while moving around the world.

This book is essentially a distillation of everything that works for us, and everything I've learnt from the other digital nomads I talked to while writing this book. It won't *all* be relevant to you – if you're a freelancer, you can skip the chapters on hiring and managing, for example – and you may not agree with all of it. But I think and hope you'll find enough in here to make it a worthwhile and helpful read.

Thanks for reading!

Mish

mish@makingitanywhere.com

p.s. If you want to read about planning for your trip (booking flights and accommodation, figuring out visas and insurance, etc.), that's all covered in my other book: **Travel Like A Pro: road-tested tips for digital nomads and frequent travelers:** www.worktravel.co/protravel.

What does this lifestyle look like?

Here's what it looks like to us:

We move to a new country every six weeks or so – sometimes slightly more, sometimes less. And once we're there, we live our "regular" lives: we work, have meetings, go out for dinner, do exercise, shop for groceries, and so on. We don't go to an office: we flit between our apartment, wifi cafes, and – thanks to data tethering – anywhere we like outdoors too.

For us, the thrill comes from both the freedom of this lifestyle and the fact that we're always somewhere new. We get to experience local life in multiple cities with exciting, different cultures. We learn about and better understand people from other countries because we live in their buildings, use their supermarkets, travel on their buses and deal with whatever political issues they're having at that moment (garbage strikes in Madrid, anti-government protests in Bangkok, marches against the stop-and-frisk policy in NYC...). We look at and learn from the various ways that they go about living their lives.

By moving around, we never get a chance to habituate to our surroundings: we're constantly experiencing and noticing everything around us. This has actually been incredibly beneficial for our businesses: it's helped us to be more creative with our ideas and solutions to our problems.

Other digital nomads don't move around quite so much: they might stay put in a city or country for months at a time. Some people even have a "base" where they spend a large chunk of the year, but will frequently take trips to other parts of the world. What makes them digital nomads is the fact that they make use of their freedom and flexibility to relocate whenever they want to – and that they're able to take their work with them.

What your digital nomad lifestyle looks like is up to you, but if you plan on moving country or city *too* frequently, you'll struggle to get much done in the way of work.

Any kind of movement between two locations requires time and energy:

- Researching where to go next

- Booking flights and accommodation

- "Flight days", when it's harder to get stuff done

- Getting to grips with your new accommodation and area

Even if you get all this down to a fine art, there's a good chance you'll still be pretty unproductive if you're moving every week or so. It's a struggle to get into a routine, and it's hard to feel like you're not missing out on everything the city has to offer if you're only there for a few days and you're meant to be working.

Which chapters should you read?

This book has been written with three types of reader in mind.

If you run a business or are about to start one up, Chapters 1, 2, 3, 4, 6 and 7 will come in most useful for you.

If you're a freelancer or about to become one, check out Chapters 1, 2, 3, 4 and 5. (And if you're thinking of sub-contracting out some aspects of your work, you might also want to read Chapters 6 and 7.)

If you're a remote worker or about to become one (i.e. you work as an employee for a company, but they allow you to do so from wherever you want to live), read Chapters 1, 2, 3 and 4. You could also read the section of Chapter 5 called "Dealing with logistics".

Note: certain tips and tools apply to more than one chapter, so you might come across the same information a couple of times (if you're reading the book in its entirety). I've marked those sections with

"Repetition alert!" so that you know which bits to skim or skip.

All readers: you'll also find a **bonus chapter: Travel Like A Pro.** This contains excerpts from my book, Travel Like A Pro (www.worktravel.co/protravel), and you'll find tips on booking flights, frequent flyer miles, visas, insurance and survival airport.

And on top of all *that,* there's an **Appendix of interviews with other digital nomads** who have a wide variety of careers and many different ways of making this lifestyle work for them. Included in this Appendix is a series of interviews with parents who travel while they work; they provide fantastic insights into how to do all this while raising children.

A note on the resources mentioned in this book

I've linked to many useful resources throughout this book; they're the ones we use regularly and wholeheartedly recommend. But new websites, online services and apps come out *the whole bloomin' time.* And while this book will be updated regularly, it may sometimes be the case that a superior alternative to an existing product emerges as soon as I hit "Publish".

If you're ever concerned that any of my recommendations have been one-upped by something newer and better, a bit of Googling will help you discover if it's worth looking into – and I hope that my initial recommendation will have at least set you on the right path to discovering something really cool and useful.

Before we get started... want free stuff?

Register your purchase of this book at www.worktravel.co for lots of free extra resources!

- A Google Doc checklist of the key "to do" items mentioned in **Chapter 1: Settle In Fast.**

- A detailed explanation of everything you want from an apartment (before you book it).

- The document we send clients before we even get on the phone with them.

- A case study of how we use Trello (a project management tool) to organise one of our projects.

- The job posting we used to hire the best staff for our distributed team.

- An SOP for setting up a job application form and collecting responses.

- An explainer video showing how to make and receive international phone calls for hardly any money – without using the internet! (Handy for if you have dodgy wifi or your clients aren't great with technology.)

Chapter 1: Settle In Fast

When you're working, you don't want to sacrifice a load of work time faffing around with getting settled and sorted: you ideally want to make your first few days in a new city as productive as any other day.

(And if you're anything like me, you don't enjoy feeling a bit lost and out of your depth when you arrive somewhere new: you want to feel at home and in control as soon as possible.)

In order to get settled and down to work ASAP, it's all just a case of working through some to-do lists…

Before you arrive

Yup – it all starts before you've even jumped on the plane!

There's lots of information and ideas in this section, but it will actually save you time by making you more efficient once you're there.

And bear in mind that you don't *have* to do it all: you can just pick the bits that are important to you. Alternatively, you could even get an assistant to do a lot of it on your behalf: just send them a checklist of everything you need.

> I've created a pre-filled (yet editable) Google Doc checklist of the key "to do" items in this chapter. Simply register your purchase of this book at www.worktravel.co to get it!
>
> (You only need to register once for all the free bonuses I've mentioned throughout this book.)

Your new apartment

Almost all the time, Rob and I will book accommodation in advance through Airbnb. In certain regions (like South East Asia and South America), many people choose to book a hostel for a couple of nights and go out looking for serviced apartments when they arrive – which is possible because those types of apartment are plentiful and cheap there. While this method is less compatible with getting down to work, it's a viable option and might be worth considering.

Whichever method you choose, make sure you know which amenities and features to look out for before you say yes to any apartment!

> For a detailed explanation of everything you want from an apartment (before you book it), register your purchase of this book at www.worktravel.co.

If you've booked a place in advance (e.g. using Airbnb), here are some extra things you can figure out before you arrive, to save time and hassle once you get there:

- Ask the host about connecting to the wifi: will they be sending you the network and password in advance, or will it be written down somewhere when you arrive?

- If you're travelling with a partner or friend... ask the host for two sets of keys to be provided. (It's amazing how many hosts only provide one set – no matter how many guests there are.)

- Store the address of your apartment (as well as any other useful contact details) in your phone, *offline*. I keep all the info in Google Keep (www.worktravel.co/keep). That way, even if something goes wrong with my phone data – or if I don't *have* any data yet – I have all the info I need when we land at the destination airport or train station. (Google Keep syncs all your notes across all your devices, but it's always available offline too. You can also use Evernote, but I find Evernote a bit too cumbersome and unnecessary for short little notes like this one.)

- Likewise, store an *offline* map of your address and the surrounding area to your phone. With offline maps, you'll still be able to see your location (the little blue dot) on the map, because your phone will use its inbuilt GPS to figure out where you are. Offline maps come in handy even if you're able to buy a SIM card as soon as you arrive: you won't use up any valuable data, and you can take day trips to other countries and find your way around.

- Google Maps allows some countries to be downloaded for offline use – here's a list of them: www.worktravel.co/offlinemaps. Here are instructions on how to download a Google Map: www.worktravel.co/offlinemaps2. There are a few disadvantages to using offline Google Maps though – namely that you can't search for points of interest or get directions to a specific place.

- If an offline Google Map isn't available for your destination country (or if you want your map to have a bit more functionality), use OsmAnd (www.worktravel.co/osmand) – a phone app for offline mapping, which also offers turn-by-turn navigation and an offline point-of-interest database. There are lots of other offline maps out there (and some people say they like Here Maps – www.worktravel.co/here), but I always come back to OsmAnd.

• Figure out how to get from the airport to your apartment in advance. If it's a train, what's the exact route – and how do you buy tickets? If it's a cab, do you need exact change? Should you steer clear of certain cab companies? Etc.

Your new area and public transportation

Wandering around and exploring is mega fun – and it's one of the major benefits of travelling while you work. But when you arrive somewhere new knowing that this *isn't* a vacation – and that your metaphorical (I hope) in-tray is piling up – you'll want to get to grips with your surrounding area as soon as possible.

"Getting to grips with the area" starts before you even travel there. Here are some things you can do:

1: Use Google Maps (www.worktravel.co/gmaps) to find the nearest grocery store, coffee shop, train station, bus stop, and anything else that's important to you. (You could also use Foursquare or Yelp to find such places and see if they've been recommended by others.) Store them as "favourites" so that they're always visible to you whenever you enter Google Maps. Here are instructions on how to save favourites: www.worktravel.co/mapfaves.

2: Change the "Home" address in Google Maps. (It'll make it a lot easier when you want to get walking or public transportation directions: just put "Home" in the "To" or "From" field. It also means there'll be a permanent "Home" icon whenever you go into Google Maps – helping you to orient yourself.)

3: Learn about your public transportation options.

- First of all, is there a transportation method that's considered "best" in that city, or optimal for certain travel situations? Wikitravel often has some great insights.

- Wikitravel also provides guidance on how to buy transportation tickets, where to get them from, which methods of transport they're valid for, and so on. The information isn't always 100% up-to-date though, so once you know the names of the transportation options, you can do some further Googling for current prices and information. (Usually you'll end up on the website of the city's public transportation provider.)

- Where's your nearest train station/bus stop/tram stop, what line is it on, and where can you travel to from it? If you want to get a good overview of your nearest stop and where it connects to, your best bet for this sort of information is to download a map from the city's public transportation website. To find the relevant map, search for "[type of transport] map [city]". So for example "tram map Prague". The city's public transportation website will usually appear first or second in the search results.

    If you just want to know how to get from your place to somewhere else in the city, use Google Maps Directions (www.worktravel.co/directions). Or the city's transportation website will often have public transportation directions there, too. (Be aware that Google Maps often doesn't contain information on all the kinds of public transportation in one city, so it may not send you on the most efficient route. For example, it doesn't contain U-Bahn information for Berlin, so never suggests it as a route option.)

- If you're not quite sure where you live in relation to the transportation map (because it's often just a network map rather than a realistic map), look out for something on the map to orient you – like a river or an airport. Train stations are often visible in Google Maps, so you could try looking there to find your nearest station. With Airbnb, the description of the listing often contains the nearest transportation stops. If it doesn't, ask your host.

4: Learn about your taxi options. In some cities it can be cheaper or much simpler to take a taxi than public transportation. Before you use one, find out from Wikitravel if you need to be aware of any taxi scams, and which taxi companies are the most widely trusted.

You can also make use of a number of taxi apps. For example:

- Uber (www.worktravel.co/uber) currently operates in cities in 55 countries. Here's the full list: www.worktravel.co/ubercities.

  Note: if you use the link www.worktravel.co/uber to sign up to Uber, you'll get a free ride (worth up to about $15).

- My Taxi (www.worktravel.co/mytaxi) does the same thing as Uber, but has presence in Spain – where Uber is currently banned.

- There's also Lyft (www.worktravel.co/lyft), but that currently only operates in certain US cities.

- Gett (www.worktravel.co/gett) is similar to Lyft and

Uber, but the pricing remains consistent (there's no "surge pricing", and you can book cabs in advance. Gett currently operates in the USA, UK, Israel and Russia – but many other countries are coming on board soon.

- There are also city-specific taxi apps; have a search for "taxi app [city]" and see what comes up (or ask a local).

You might find yourself on a lot of foreign websites throughout all this. They'll almost always have an English language option, but if they don't you can use Google Chrome's built-in website translator or go to the Google Translate website (www.worktravel.co/gtranslate): copy and paste the URL of that website into the box.

Money

In **Chapter 2: Get To Grips With Money And Taxes**, there's more information about bank accounts, credit cards, debit cards, alternative forms of payment, and ATMs. This is just a mini-section about preparing for a new currency and a (perhaps) different way of spending it than you're used to – because goodness knows we've been caught out by such seemingly simple things as "buying stuff at the supermarket".

Here are a few things you could prepare for before you travel:

- **Download a currency-conversion app.** And find a way to memorise the basic conversion rate for small, ad-hoc purchases. XE (www.worktravel.co/xe) provides apps for a wide range of devices.

- **Set up an alert/reminder to get cash out of the ATM as soon as you arrive at the airport or station.** In many countries, it's likely you'll need to pay for something in cash before you arrive at your location. (Also, you won't know where the ATMs are near your new home.)

    Pro tip: Google Keep (www.worktravel.co/keep) has location-based alerts, which means you can set it to sound an alarm as soon as you arrive at the airport.

- **Use Numbeo (www.worktravel.co/numbeo) to find out how much things SHOULD cost in the city.** That way, you won't pay 2,000 Thai baht for a cab ride from the airport (even if you have no clue what that is in your home currency) because you'll know it should be about 300 Thai baht.

Language

We know a small minority of digital nomads who'll wander into a cafe in whichever country they're in and order their drink in English without so much as saying "Hello" in the country's language. To me, this just seems incredibly rude – particularly in cities that aren't so touristy, but even in areas where they're used to speaking English to tourists.

If I worked as a waitress in London and someone came in and immediately asked "¿Puedo tomar una taza de té?" I'd be appalled. At the very least they could say "Hello" in English and then politely enquire as to whether I speak Spanish.

I know it's not realistic to suggest that people who travel and work should learn the language of every country. I certainly don't do that. In fact, I'm a quivering, juddery, nervous wreck whenever I try to say *anything* in a different language. But I think it's important to learn the basics and ingratiate yourself to whomever you're dealing with. Even just saying "Hello" and "Do you speak English?" in their language shows that you're trying and you're willing.

Rant over. Now onto the practicalities of how to do this...

- **Use Google Translate (www.worktravel.co/gtranslate) to translate a few key words and phrases** ("hello", "goodbye", "do you speak English?", "delicious!", etc.). You can hear how they sound by clicking on the "speaker" symbol.

- If you want to practise these words, **use a flashcard app** like Anki (www.worktravel.co/anki).

- **If you actually want to have a go at learning the language, Duolingo (www.worktravel.co/duolingo) should be your first port of call.** It's a language-learning and crowdsourced text-translation platform, available in a number of languages. It's gamified, free, and immensely fun – so it ticks all the boxes. You may end up being asked to translate phrases like "The bear will not fit through the door" and "My yellow turtles drink milk", but you *will* learn how to speak the language.

Also give Michel Thomas audiobooks a try: www.worktravel.co/michel.

And there are a number of language-learning podcasts available on iTunes.

- **To get to grips with how language is spoken in everyday life and written in everyday text...**

    - Download some kids' TV programmes in that language. The speaking is slower and simpler than regular TV shows.

    - OTT soap operas (think foreign versions of Days Of Our Lives) are also a great idea – and it's how Rob upped his Spanish proficiency while also getting excited about how the guy who Carmela drugged and framed for her sister's murder was actually an undercover FBI agent all along.

If you're in the mood for geeking out over Google Translate (www.worktravel.co/gtranslate), the phone app has many extra functions and uses (some of these are Android only):

- **Offline languages.** Go into the settings, then "manage offline languages", then you can click on the pin icon next to any language to download the entire dictionary for offline use. So as long as you've planned ahead, you can start translating as soon as you arrive without having to find wifi or sort out a local data connection.

- **Translate from camera.** Tap the camera icon to take a photo of any text (a menu, perhaps) and have the entire thing translated for you – which is so much quicker than doing it word-by-word. You do need data access for this, though.

- **Speak and translate.** Speak in your own language and Google Translate will display the translation, then the other person just taps on their own language to speak back to you. You can therefore have a complete Google-mediated conversation with someone – all you need is to trust Google's speech recognition not to mishear you and end up accidentally insulting their mother.

- **Make full screen.** Once you've translated a word or phrase, you can just go into the options and tap "make full screen" to show someone what you want to say without sending them scrambling for their reading glasses.

- **Save to phrasebook.** Tapping the star icon next to a translation will save it to your phrasebook, which synchronises across all your devices – so you can keep common phrases (like "Co ve jménu svaté sakra je s vaší Wifi v pořádku") at hand for when you need them.

Culture, customs and ways of doing things

Learning about the culture and customs of a city or country isn't just important for showing respect; it'll also help you feel more at home more quickly.

Here are some things you might want to look into before you travel to your next destination:

- How does tipping work – how much do you tip (if anything), who do you tip, and how do you tip? There are a few global tipping apps on the market, like GlobeTipping for iPhone (www.worktravel.co/globetipping) and Global Tip Calculator Pro for Android (www.worktravel.co/globalpro). Wikitravel also has tipping information for lots of countries.

- How do people greet each other?

- What's the etiquette when using public transport?

- What are the meal times – and are restaurants open outside these times?

- Which religion (or philosophy) is the most widely practised – and are there any rules/observances you should be aware of relating to that religion?

- What times and days are the shops open?

- What actions or words are frowned upon? (For example, in Thailand you can go to prison for saying anything negative about the royal family, you should never point with one finger, and you shouldn't walk into someone's home with your shoes on.)

You can usually find out a lot about these things on Wikitravel, and by Googling "customs etiquette [name of country]".

SIM cards

If you learn in advance which SIM card to get for your destination country, it'll mean you can usually buy the SIM card at the airport. Bonus advantage: the staff at the airport store are more likely to speak English and help you with setting up the card on your phone.

Prepaid SIMs (as opposed to contracts or PAYG) are the way forward if you move around the world a lot:

- You know exactly what you're paying, because you pay a month at a time upfront for a package of minutes, texts and data. The SIM provider doesn't have your card details, so you know that you won't get charged anything on top of what you've already paid.

- You can often pay for subsequent months online.

- You're not tied into a long-term contract.

In most countries, you'll have a lot of prepaid SIM options to choose from – and it's difficult to know which one is best for your needs. Here's a step-by-step process for helping you figure it out:

- Google the following: "[country] monthly prepaid SIM

3G [current year]". ("3G" because I'm going to assume that data is important to you and you'll want it included as part of your plan. Many countries don't yet have 4G. "[current year]" so that you get up-to-date information.)

- Find any forums or authoritative sites that talk about it. DON'T look at any individual SIM card provider sites that appear in the search results.

- Compile a list of the SIM providers at your destination that seem to provide prepaid monthly plans. Then to find your ideal prepaid plan, do some more research into those providers. Here's what you'll need to know:

    - Is it easy to find stores in the destination country where you can buy the SIM card and prepaid plan? (At the airport, local stores, the mall...)

    - Once you have your SIM card, can you pay for subsequent months online (rather than go into a shop)? This may or may not be important to you.

    - Is it possible to buy "add-ons" to your prepaid plan (like international calls)? Again: this may or may not be important to you.

    - Will the SIM card work with your phone?

    - What's the coverage like in your part of the country?

    - How do you activate the new SIM card once it's

in your phone? (A person at the store will often do it for you, but if not, you might want to look online for instructions – just in case the instructions on the packet are in a different language.)

- Does the SIM allow tethering, so that you can share your phone's internet connection with your laptop? Not all SIM cards allow this, but it's a useful thing to have because it means you'll be able to work even if you arrive at your apartment and the wifi happens to be shoddy.

As well as using the above instructions, you might want to check out the following websites for their crowd-sourced info on SIM packages around the world (bear in mind that the info might be incomplete or out of date):

- **TripAdvisor forum** (www.worktravel.co/taforum): click on the country you're interested in, then type something like "monthly prepaid SIM 3G".

- **Prepaid with Data** (www.worktravel.co/prepaid): a massively useful resource, but it often doesn't have all the information/available packages for each SIM card provider. Also, the information is presented in a way that's often a bit difficult to understand. You're best off using this site as a way to find a list of SIM providers in each country – and then you can use that list to do further research.

- Lonely Planet forum (www.worktravel.co/planetforum): often has useful Q&As about SIMs around the world.

Shopping lists

You *may* think this is overkill – and you may indeed be right – but Rob and I write a shopping list before we get to a new destination, so that we can arrive at the apartment, check if there are any "essentials" like salt, soap, etc. already available (in which case we'll strike them off the list), then head straight out to the supermarket to buy everything and get settled.

We tend to buy just the basics the first time – the stuff that we know is available in most supermarkets around the world like bread, oats, fish, meat, vegetables and fruit. We'll then stock up on more adventurous goodies another time.

(We don't do any of this in Southeast Asia because we tend to buy a lot of street food – but we find it useful for the rest of the world.)

I use the Google Keep's "checklists" functionality (www.worktravel.co/keep) to write out the list – and then I can check everything off as we're walking around the store.

Once you're there

All the prep work you've done before you arrive will make *being there* a breeze: you'll already have your bearings, know what SIM card you need, know where the nearest supermarket is, and so on. You'll adjust and get settled in no time – especially once you've read the next section and sorted out your mail, your friends, your fitness and your food and drink.

The first few hours

Here's a list of all the things you can do to get yourself organised and settled within the first few hours of arriving somewhere new:

At the airport

- Get cash out of the ATM

- Buy a SIM card (if possible)

At your apartment

- Connect to the wifi

- Find the fuse box*

- Unpack and figure out where everything is

- Do a stock check and add/remove items from your shopping list if necessary

- Check that the shower works how you expect it to (you don't want to realise you can't use it when you're stark naked and sweaty from a run)

- Take photos (with dates) of anything that looks a bit broken or damaged: you don't want to get blamed for those later

*This is not a ridiculous suggestion, I promise: the fuse has blown in more apartments than I can remember – and if we didn't know where the fuse box was beforehand, we certainly struggled to find it in the pitch black.

Out and about

These suggestions might be a tad on the obvious side, but what the hey: they're short at least!

- Buy a SIM card (if you weren't able to earlier)

- Go grocery shopping

- Get your bearings

And you're all set!

Restaurants, bars and local attractions

We have a rule of thumb in our (various) household(s): when it comes to eating and drinking out, ignore TripAdvisor.

If you want to eat authentic cuisine, drink where all the locals drink and avoid being ripped off, your best bet is to ask someone who's local to the area (like your Airbnb host) and who knows what they're talking about. If that's not an option, try out some of the websites where locals and longer-term residents will review the restaurants, bars and off-the-beaten-track attractions. These sites are by no means perfect, but they'll often give you a much better picture of a place than TripAdvisor (which is used by tourists).

Here are a few suggestions:

- Foursquare (www.worktravel.co/foursquare) is popular throughout Europe.

- Yelp (www.worktravel.co/yelp) is most useful in the US.

- Spotted By Locals (www.worktravel.co/spotted) provides recommendations for food and attractions by locals in 61 countries throughout Europe and North America.

- Tabelog (www.worktravel.co/tabelog) is widely used in Japan. The site has an English-language version so you can search for restaurants in English, then see the ratings and photos. Google Translate works pretty well on the Japanese reviews.

- Vayable (www.worktravel.co/vayable) provides a marketplace where locals offer unique tours (including lots of food-related tours) to visitors.

Receive mail

If you want to order anything online and get it delivered, you'll need to find out if it's possible to receive letters or parcels at your apartment. Many apartment buildings have small mailboxes for each apartment in the lobby area, but the Airbnb host/landlord often keeps hold of the key.

If the parcel is delivered by a courier but you're not particularly au fait with the language, you may struggle to understand or be understood through the intercom system. And even if you *do* have a grasp of the language, you might be out when they deliver – and you have no proof of address to collect the parcel from the mail centre or arrange a redelivery.

So it might be worthwhile looking into other methods for receiving mail. Here are some options:

- **Post Restante.** This is a service where the post office holds mail until you go in to collect it. In the words of Wikipedia, it's a "common destination for mail for people who are visiting a particular location and have no need, or no way, of having mail delivered directly to their place of residence at the time." Visit the Wikipedia page for more information on how to use it in your particular country: www.worktravel.co/post. And if your country isn't on the list, a bit of Googling should reveal everything you need to know.

- **Amazon Lockers** (US and UK only). These are a self-service parcel delivery service offered by Amazon. You select any Locker location as the delivery address (they're often located inside grocery and convenience stores), and pick up your order at that location by entering a unique pick-up code on the Locker touch screen. Find out more here: www.worktravel.co/locker.

- **Amazon Pickup Points** (various countries). You can choose to have your Amazon orders sent to a local store like a post office or convenience store, which you can then go and pick up at a time that suits you (you'll need ID). Google "Amazon Pickup Point [name of city]" to find out if the service is available at your destination.

- **Various pickup lockers run by various companies.** DHL Packstations in Germany (www.worktravel.co/packstation), Doddle in the UK (www.worktravel.co/doddle), My Pick Box in Spain (www.worktravel.co/pickup)... Have a Google around for "pickup locker [location]", "delivery locker [location]", "collect parcel from store [location]" and so on.

- **Parcel** (Manhattan and parts of Brooklyn only): www.worktravel.co/parcel. This is incredible: get all your parcels shipped to a special unique address at Parcel HQ, and schedule them to arrive (by courier) at your apartment during a one-hour slot of your choice in the evening. There are bound to be similar services around the world soon, so keep an eye out!

But what if you have a "home" address somewhere in the world, and important mail (like bank cards or invoices) gets sent there? How do you make sure you get hold of that mail while you're living somewhere else entirely for a few months?

Well... you *could* ask a friend or relative to pop over every so often and pick up the mail. But if you're renting out your place or your friend/relative isn't as delighted to do the favour as you'd hoped, there's still another workaround: a mail-forwarding service. Here's how it works:

1. Sign up to a mail-forwarding service in your home country, at which point you'll be given a unique address at one of their locations.

2. Inform the post office in your home country of a change of address (or say that you'd like your mail to be redirected until x date).

3. The mail-forwarding service will receive your mail, scan it and upload the scan to your online dashboard. You can then decide whether you want that mail forwarded on to wherever you happen to be living, or if it's enough to see the mail's contents over a scan.

You usually get billed monthly, and then there are different fee structures for scanning, delivering and shredding your mail.

Here are some mail-forwarding services around the world (there are plenty of others, so be sure to do some Googling around and compare the features and prices of the ones available to you):

- In the UK, we use UK Postbox: www.worktravel.co/ukpost.

- In the USA, Earth Class Mail is popular: www.worktravel.co/earthclass.

- Germany has ClevverMail: www.worktravel.co/clevver.

- Australians can use Aussie Mail Man: www.worktravel.co/aussie. You'll be given a PO Box address as default, but you can pay extra for a residential address.

Watch your favourite TV shows

You'll find that many on-demand TV services you use in your home country will refuse you access (or only show you a restricted catalogue) when you're abroad. You can get around this by using a VPN, which makes it appear like your device is in a different country.

Some TV services have got wise to the VPN trick and block traffic that they know originates from an IP address associated with a particular VPN (Hulu in particular is very "on it" when it comes to this sort of thing), so you might want to look into what others have to say about any VPN before you start using it (Google "[name of VPN] [name of TV service]"). Paid VPN services – where you pay a monthly or yearly subscription and get your own individual IP address rather than a shared one – are less likely to be on their radars than free services – and they also tend to be a lot faster.

My recommended VPN: TorGuard (www.worktravel.co/torguard).

We've tried out a LOT of VPNs over the years, and TorGuard is the best. It costs $9.99 a month (or $29.99 for six months paid upfront*), but it's worth it:

- It's way faster than the free VPNs: you won't have to amuse yourself 50 times a minute while your TV show buffers.

- It allows up to five connections per account – which means you can install it on your computer, your partner's computer, both your smartphones and your iPad.

- It always seems to work perfectly. (We've used so many services in the past – even paid ones – where the service fails to connect, or drops out halfway through.)

- It has servers in about 40 countries, which means you'll be able to watch TV shows online from countries as wide-ranging as the UK, USA, Canada, Australia, Egypt, Germany, Mexico, Moldova, Latvia and India.

- The customer service is excellent.

*It's also $59.99 if you pay for a whole year, which is, erm, exactly double what you'd pay for the six-month rate. I'm not quite sure what the benefit is there.

Read **Chapter 3: Guard Your Data** for more about the security benefits of using a VPN.

Find other digital nomads

A couple of years ago we spent two months in Berlin – at the same time that (by pure and happy coincidence) lots of other digital nomads were living there too. While we were there, our business was a mess: we were frantic with worry about finding enough clients, making enough money, and doing enough of a good job.

But we still have fond memories of that summer in Berlin, because hanging around with the other nomads made us realise very quickly that these were *our people*. We clicked with them, they got us, we understood each other.

We've experienced the same thing again and again with our digital nomad friends around the world. And I think it's because there's one big thing (often the *only* thing) that we all have in common: we've all chosen to opt out of the regular way of living our lives. We've removed ourselves from peer pressure. We've chosen to do things *our* way – a way that's quite unlike "the norm".

And all this means that anything goes – with a level of acceptance that we haven't found with other friendship groups. If we leave a Sunday lunch early to get some work done, it's totally normal – as is the fact that some of our friends won't hang out before midday because they have calls with US clients until 4am. Everyone just does their thing, and everyone else is fine with it.

There's also a certain kind of honesty and unselfconsciousness that we've never found before. If someone suggests going to a bar, it's acceptable to say "I don't drink – shall we go for a walk instead?" without the risk of being thought of as weird or uncool. And if the rest of the group wants to go waterskiing, there's minimal shame in saying you'll sit it out out because you got a bit queasy on the Disney teacup ride as a kid and never quite bounced back.

It feels incredible to find friends who really get you – where you can completely be yourself, there's no pressure to conform or be judged, and the inconvenient placement of power outlets in Airbnb apartments is acceptable dinner conversation.

There are, however, two drawbacks to having digital nomad friends:

1. You won't be able to take the same group of friends with you wherever you go.

2. It's not the easiest thing in the world to find these people in the first place (after all, it's not like you grew up with them or work with them).

Assuming that you can deal with the first point (because there's not much else you *can* do if you want this lifestyle), there are a few methods by which you can find new digital nomad friends while you travel the world. Here are some of them:

- **Put your pin on the Find A Nomad (www.worktravel.co/findanomad) map.** There's a bit more information about Find A Nomad in the next section.

- Create Your Nomadtopia (www.worktravel.co/topia) is a fab Facebook group. (You need to ask for permission to join.)

- Follow other digital nomad blogs and – if you like the writers – let them know if you're in the same area as them.

- Twitter-stalk people and see where they are/where they're heading.

- If you have any digital nomad buddies already, ask them if they can introduce you (virtually) to others so that you can go on to meet them (in person) when you're both in the same place.

- Search for "digital nomad" on Meetup.com.

- Go to a coworking space and get talking to other people there. (Search Google for "coworking [name of city". There are also a number of coworking directories, like ShareDesk (www.worktravel.co/sharedesk).

About Find A Nomad

Find A Nomad (www.worktravel.co/findanomad) is the scratch that we created for our very own itch: an easy way to find other digital nomads within the city in which we're living or the city in which we *will* be living soon.

We created Find A Nomad alongside our online community The Anywhereist Group (www.worktravel.co/anywhereist) – which happens to be another great way to meet people!

Find A Nomad is a completely free tool for discovering where friends and potential new friends are right now – and where they'll be throughout the year.

When you arrive somewhere new, you can see (on a map) who's in town. You can click to view their profile and find out more about them, and then send them a message if you'd like to meet up. You can even plan your future travels around where your friends and other interesting people are going to be – because all users are able to add the dates of their upcoming trips too.

At the time of writing, over 1,500 digital nomads are using Find A Nomad. You can join them for free by signing up at www.worktravel.co/findanomad.

Stay fit

It's tough to have a fitness routine if you're only staying in places for a couple of months at a time: if you're a jogger, you have to learn the layout of a whole new city and get your bearings. If you used to have a gym membership, it's hard to find gyms in cities that will allow you to take out short-term membership. And if you're a fan of team-based exercises, it isn't exactly easy to find a local team where you can get involved and understand what's going on.

So yes… keeping fit is harder to do when you're travelling while working! But there ARE ways to do it. Here are some ideas:

Running, walking and cycling outside

When you arrive in a new city, you don't know your way around – which makes it daunting to go out for a run or cycle without any sort of map to hand. Even if you go out with Google Maps on your phone, it's a bit of an effort to constantly be checking where you are, how far away from home you are, and which route to take back again.

Here's what I do to make it all much easier:

- I have OsmAnd (www.worktravel.co/osmand) – an offline map app – installed on my phone. Through OsmAnd I download the offline map for whichever country I'm in.

- I create a route around whichever city I'm in using Ride With GPS (www.worktravel.co/gps). I then export that route as a .gpx file.

- I hook my phone up to my computer, then transfer the .gpx file to the "tracks" folder inside my OsmAnd app.

- I can then view the map and the route on my phone, even without data.

    Here's how to view the route on your phone:

    - Go to the map of whichever city you're in, then click on the "Settings" button at the bottom of the screen.

- Click "My Places" and hold down your .gpx route until a menu appears.

- Click "Show on map". The map with a route will show on the map.

- Click the "Settings" button on the screen again, and choose "Directions".

All I have to do then is follow the blue arrow and the big purple line on my screen. I'm able to memorise the route after about three days of doing it, and after that I no longer need to use my phone. (I then usually switch up my route every couple of weeks or so.)

Extra tip: you could buy a phone case with a lanyard, so that you don't have to hold your phone the whole time. Like this one: www.worktravel.co/lanyard.

Indoor exercising

Turns out there are a lot of exercises that you can do in small apartments without any equipment – and they won't annoy the neighbours, either. Everything listed here is a video-based workout, because I think they're more engaging than a list of instructions and/or diagrams.

- **Fitness Blender** (www.worktravel.co/blender) provides full-length workout videos for every fitness level, absolutely free. (It's funded by advertising, donations and paid-for workout programs.) All the videos are music-free – the idea being that you play whichever music you like instead.

The great thing about Fitness Blender is the ability to filter down to the type of workout you want. You can filter by length of workout, calories burned, training type, equipment needed, and so on. If you type "apartment" in the keyword search box, you'll see all the apartment-friendly workouts – i.e. the ones that don't involve jumping or jogging and won't annoy whoever's living downstairs.

- **DDP Yoga** (www.worktravel.co/ddp) is run by "Diamond" Dallas Page, a retired professional wrestler. While DDP is inspired by regular yoga, it contains – in his words – a "secret sauce" (dynamic resistance) to increase your heart rate and burn more fat.

    You can buy DDP Yoga "packs" starting at $65 from the website. (Annoyingly, everything is on DVD.)

- **Do You Yoga** (www.worktravel.co/yoga) is led by the wonderful Erin, who's funny, laid back, and makes you feel like you can *nail* this yoga malarky. Her free 30-Day Yoga Challenge (www.worktravel.co/challenge) has been a huge hit, and it's a great way to find out if her teaching style is for you. Beyond that, there are many other reasonably priced courses on the site. You don't need any equipment, but a yoga mat wouldn't go amiss.

- **Focus T25** (www.worktravel.co/t25) may just kill you. Created by fitness trainer and former Mariah Carey backup dancer Shaun T, it's a high-intensity cardio/strength training program that lasts 25 minutes. It replaces the longer "Insanity" fitness program you might have heard of, but promises to give the same results.

    There's a fair bit of noise-making in the form of jumping and jogging, but Shaun T offers you lower-impact alternatives if you're worried about the neighbours.

    Prices are all over the place for different packages, but they tend to start at about $39.95 (and again, it's all on DVD).

- **Sleek Technique** (www.worktravel.co/sleek) was recommended to me by a Making It Anywhere reader, and I love it! It consists of total fitness workouts based on ballet techniques – which are tougher than you might expect.

    You can take a free taster class on YouTube: www.worktravel.co/sleekfree. For more classes, you can pay £30 a month for unlimited access to all the workouts on the website and one free live class, or £48 for that plus unlimited access to all live classes. There's also a Pay As You Go option.

    The only equipment you'll need is a chair or table (to act as a barre) and sometimes a mat.

Gyms

Some gyms around the world will let you pay by the month or by the week (or even by the day) without penalty. For advice on where to find them, head to Nomad Forum (www.worktravel.co/nomadforum) and search for "gym [name of city]". If nothing shows up, ask the question yourself! Nomad Forum is very active, and someone's bound to answer.

Alternatively, you could of course just do a Google search; try "gym monthly [name of city]". Or see if there are any Facebook groups for expats in your city; join one and ask in there.

Free community fitness

Just before publishing this book, a blog reader sent me this advice:

"When travelling, I've found '[city] free early morning workout' to be a good Google search to do. The people who are prepared to get up early and workout outside probably have a similar outlook on life as you, plus you get your exercise done early doors."

In London he recommends Project Awesome (www.worktravel.co/awesome) – "a community fitness drive offering upbeat classes for Londoners for free".

In the States, there's November Project (www.worktravel.co/november) – "a free fitness movement that was born in Boston as a way to stay in shape during cold New England months. Now present in multiple cities in across four time zones in North

America."

As well as searching Google for similar groups around the world, you could also look on Meetup.com for fitness meetups near where you're living.

Conclusion

Most people have to go through this process a couple of times in their entire lives; you'll be doing it a few times *a year*, at least!

Once you've cracked the whole "settling in" process, you'll love it: it's part of the thrill and excitement of being a digital nomad. Discovering amazing new restaurants and beautiful parks is *obviously* amazing, but so too is finding your way around the local supermarket, figuring out how the road crossings work, and being able to do currency conversions on demand.

For more tips on settling in fast, take a look through some of the interviews in the **Appendix**.

If you want help with the prep and planning process of travel (flights, visas, insurance, etc.), read the **bonus chapter: Travel Like A Pro** at the end of this book.

Mish Slade 50

Chapter 2: Get To Grips With Money And Taxes

Even though technology has made the world *very* easy for people who want to be digital nomads, the same can't be said for the institutions that control money and taxes.

The general gist is this:

- When you spend money abroad, there's a good chance you have to pay a whacking great transaction fee every time you withdraw money from an ATM or buy something in a store.

- It's pretty unclear how digital nomads are meant to go about reporting or paying tax correctly, because tax laws were written before it was feasible to generate income while living anywhere.

In this chapter I provide you with a bit of background information on these two issues, plus links to other relevant sources that will be more up-to-date than a book can ever be. I also explain an easy way in which you can track your spending and calculate your cost of living – which can come in useful if your money needs to go a long way (or you're just interested in how much you spend in different countries).

Note: the links I've provided in the "tax" section are based on the assumption that you're still a resident in your "home" country, even if you don't live there often. Some digital nomads move around the world in such a way that they're able to avoid being a resident of anywhere (and thus they can avoid taxes too). But these people are in the minority: becoming a "tax nomad" is difficult to achieve, and many people don't agree with it in principle.

Spending money when abroad

When you go away for a two-week holiday in the sun, you're probably not too fussed about the slightly crappy conversion rate at the Bureau de Change, or you take a "WE'RE ON VACATION!!!" approach to ATM and credit card fees. But when you're travelling between different countries full time, those fees add up and aren't so easy to swallow: withdrawing the equivalent of $100 in a foreign country could actually cost you up to $8 – sometimes more.

But it doesn't necessarily have to be this way. Next are some options to get around transaction fee hell, and then I briefly explain what *we* do when we're travelling.

Credit and debit cards

Your regular credit and debit cards can be used anywhere in the world, but you'll often be forced to pay a hefty fee every time you use them abroad.

The fee percentage will differ according to which credit card network (Visa, MasterCard, etc.) you're using and who the issuing bank is (Bank of America, NatWest, RBC, etc.), but here's how the fees break down:

Withdrawing money from an ATM (debit card)

- **ATM fee**: the fee that your bank charges you for withdrawing money from an ATM in a foreign country (even if it's an ATM that belongs to your bank). The amount varies, but many banks charge up to the equivalent (in your currency) of $5.

    You also might be charged a separate fee by the ATM operator itself.

- **Transaction fee (also called a load fee)**: a combined fee (charged by your bank and card network) for withdrawing money in a foreign currency and converting it into your home currency using the day's wholesale exchange rate*. It's usually about 3% of the value of what you're withdrawing.

    Note: most ATM operators offer to do the currency conversion for you, but the exchange rates they offer are usually sucky. You're often better off accepting your bank's transaction fee and the wholesale exchange rate instead.

Spending money using a debit or credit card

- **Transaction fee (sometimes called a foreign purchase fee or a load fee):** a combined fee (charged by your bank and card network) for spending money in a foreign currency and converting it into your home currency using the day's wholesale exchange rate*. It's usually about 3%.

    Note: at the checkout, you might be offered the choice between being charged in the foreign currency (which is when your bank's transaction fee applies) or being charged in your home currency (your bank *usually* doesn't charge for this). If you choose to be charged in your home currency, the retailer or retailer's bank will probably give you a *horrible* exchange rate and may also add on their own conversion fees, so you're better off being charged in the foreign currency and letting your bank do the conversion.

- **Spending fee:** an extra, for-the-fun-of-it fee that some banks charge you for spending with your debit card. There aren't many banks that do this, but the ones that do can charge about $2 *per purchase.*

The wholesale exchange rate is also known as the "interbank" rate. It's what banks charge each other to convert large sums of money.

The percentages may not look that scary, but they add up – especially if you're doing this full time.

Plenty of people simply take a deep breath and accept the fact that they have to pay extra for the privilege of living and working around the world. If you choose this option, a simple money-saving tactic is to ALWAYS choose to be charged or withdraw money in the local currency. See above for why.

But if you're willing to do a bit of research, there are ways to reduce your costs more significantly when using a debit or credit card. Here are some methods to consider:

Get a card that charges low fees or no fees

As mentioned earlier, when you buy or withdraw money in the local currency, your bank uses the day's wholesale exchange rate (which is the best rate you can get) and charges you a fee for converting the amount back to your home currency.

But certain banks and card providers have lower fees than others, and some will waive them entirely: they give you the wholesale exchange rate but won't charge you a fee for doing so. What's more, certain banks and card providers will also waive the ATM fee for withdrawing cash. And at least one provider will even reimburse you for any fee that the ATM itself charges you.

Here are some useful links (which are kept constantly up-to-date) for helping you figure out which cards you're eligible for:

If you're from the UK, Money Saving Expert is all you need:

- A comparison of fees from all the major UK debit card

providers: www.worktravel.co/ukdebit

- A comparison of fees from all the major UK credit card providers: www.worktravel.co/ukcredit

- A list of the best specialist travel credit cards (which don't tend to charge any transaction fees but may have other drawbacks or conditions): www.worktravel.co/uktravelcredit

- Information about travel debit cards: www.worktravel.co/uktraveldebit (note that you'd have to actually change bank if you wanted to change your debit card)

If you're from the US, try out these sites:

- Visit your bank's website to find out what fees you'll be paying on your debit and credit cards when you travel

- CreditCards.com has an up-to-date list of credit cards that don't charge a foreign transaction fee: www.worktravel.co/ustravelcredit

- Nerd Wallet has a list of all the banks and their respective debit card transaction/ATM fees: www.worktravel.co/ustraveldebit

- Nomadic Matt has some useful information about avoiding ATM and credit/debit card transaction fees: www.worktravel.co/avoidfees

- As previously mentioned, some ATMs charge their own fee – on top of the ATM fee and the transaction fee charged by your bank. If you get a Charles Schwab debit card though, you'll be reimbursed those ATM fees. That doesn't mean it's necessarily the best bank for you, of course. Find out more about it here: www.worktravel.co/schwab

If you're from Australia, take a look here:

- Finder contains some excellent information on credit/debit cards and foreign transaction fees: www.worktravel.co/finder

If you're from elsewhere in the world...

- Google the following: "foreign transaction fee credit [or debit] card". Lots and lots of useful websites will appear in the results!

The above websites are all extremely useful, but I'd recommend that you use them as starting points in your research rather than the *only* websites you have to read.

Extra tips

- When you use your credit card to withdraw money from an ATM, you'll be charged interest on that cash withdrawal until you've paid it off. It's better to withdraw money using a debit card.

- Some banks waive the ATM fee if you withdraw money

from partner bank ATMs abroad. For example, Bank of America is a member of the Global ATM Alliance. While it generally charges a $5 fee to withdraw cash from a foreign ATM, the fee will be waived if you use an ATM belonging to another Global ATM Alliance bank. A full list of Global ATM Alliance banks can be found here: www.worktravel.co/globalatm.

- If your bank *doesn't* waive the ATM fee, you're better off making a few big withdrawals rather than lots of mini-ones. That's because the fee is a set amount rather than a percentage of the amount you withdraw.

- Remember to always withdraw or pay for goods using the local currency – and let your bank do the conversion for you, even if they charge a fee for doing so. See the introduction to this section ("Credit and debit cards") for more information.

- There's a growing prevalence of "chip-and-pin" cards throughout Europe, Asia and South America. These cards rely on an embedded chip that transmits information to a merchant, which the consumer then verifies by entering a PIN. If you have a traditional card with a magnetic strip, it shouldn't be much of a problem in stores and restaurants (where someone will be able to swipe it for you), but it could be a tad trickier at ticket vending kiosks, gas stations or other places featuring automated payment machines. If possible, see if your bank will provide you with a chip-and-pin card.

The future of credit/debit cards?

A new way of banking is on the horizon – one that makes the most of advances in cloud computing, smartphones and social networking.

Check out Number26 (www.worktravel.co/26) and Supercard (www.worktravel.co/supercard) for more information. I won't write about them too much here because they're both still very new at the time of writing – and only available in Europe and the UK respectively. But they're worth keeping a close eye on because they could make transaction fees and ATM fees a thing of the past.

Prepaid travel cards

If you're old enough to remember traveller's cheques, high-fives! Prepaid travel cards are the new-fangled version of traveller's cheques: you load them up with the foreign currency of your choice before you set off, and then just use them as you would a debit card to spend or withdraw cash as you wish. They're typically linked to the Visa or MasterCard network, and they come in a wide variety of currencies.

There are also "multi-currency" cards available, which allow you to load up to nine currencies on a single card.

Prepaid travel cards have an assortment of pros and cons:

Pros:

- They're pre-loaded, which allows you to keep tight

control of your spending.

- You lock in a rate when you load, which means you won't be affected by currency fluctuations and you'll know *exactly* how much something costs you every time you spend money. (And if your currency weakens after you load the card, you can feel smug.)

    Note: this isn't always the case with multi-currency cards: some of them only apply the exchange rate when you pay for something, rather than when you load the card with that currency.

- You can load more money onto the card whenever you like (by transferring money from your bank account by phone or online), so they're a long-term solution as well as for vacationers. BUT you're normally charged a fee to reload your card.

- Like bank cards, they're protected by chip-and-pin. Unlike bank cards, however, they're not connected to your bank account or credit card account – which means that you don' have to worry about ID theft or fraudulent transactions if yours is lost or stolen.

- If your card *is* lost or stolen and you report it immediately, you can get a replacement card with any unused funds transferred (sometimes for free; sometimes for a small fee depending on the card provider). In this sense, it's far better than carrying cash around with you.

Cons:

- The fact that you lock in a currency when you load is great for your sense of certainty and knowing exactly how much something costs you, but you might feel a bit miffed if your currency strengthens and the cash on your card effectively has less buying power than if you were to simply withdraw money from your account at that moment.

- Not everywhere accepts them.

- There are fees (not all fees apply to all cards):

    - **Application and replacement fees**: around $15 to start using your prepaid card, and then a $7.50ish "replacement fee" – which some providers charge after 12 months if you want to keep using the card.

    - **Monthly "just because" fees**: that's not how they describe it, but it's what it amounts to. It's usually a few dollars.

    - **ATM fees:** a charge for every time you withdraw cash from an ATM (usually in the range of about $2).

    - **Inactivity fees:** a small monthly fee that starts to get charged if the card goes unused for 12 months.

- **Exchange rate:** most cards will use the wholesale exchange rate when you buy the currency, but add on a sneaky little margin for themselves.

  The "rate+margin" is still usually better than a debit/credit card "rate+transaction fee", but you'll want to double check to make sure (and all the other fees associated with a prepaid travel card might make it worse off in the long run).

- **Redemption fee:** a not-insignificant cost (around $15) for getting any money back that you haven't used on the card.

- **Reloading fee:** for every time you want to add more money to your card (usually around 2%).

Find the best prepaid travel cards

The offers and rates on prepaid travel cards change frequently, so you're best off scouring the internet when you're ready to buy. Google "best prepaid travel cards [denomination of currency]" and see what comes up.

When you start researching, you'll notice that there are lots of rules and stipulations around some of the best-value prepaid cards. For example, some cards allow you to get out of the monthly "just because" fee on the condition that you have a certain amount loaded onto the card at any one time, or that you make a minimum number of purchases on the card each month.

Buying currency before you travel

Here are a few reasons why you might want to actually buy currency before you arrive at your destination:

- You want to lock in a once-in-a-lifetime-amazeballs exchange rate – but you don't want to deal with all the complicated fees and restrictions that come with a prepaid travel card.

- You're lumbered with a currency that you won't need again soon, so you may as well change it for the currency of your next destination.

- You know that the country you're visiting is a bit of an ATM desert – and you want to arrive with cash rather than expect there to be a working ATM at the airport.

Buying currency in advance will rarely give you the best deal: there's always a large commission fee on top of a bad exchange rate. (If you see any adverts for places that charge "0% commission", they're simply giving you a *really bad* exchange rate rather than a bad rate plus commission.) You're pretty much always better off withdrawing the money from an ATM at your arrival destination – unless you want to have the money in advance for any of the reasons above.

Here are some ways in which you can buy currency before you arrive:

- **At an airport/station currency exchange.** Just don't: the rates are abysmal because they know you have no other options left.

- **At a high street currency exchange (including banks).** The rates are better, but not amazing. You might think you'll get a good deal if you buy currency at your own bank, but they're unlikely to give you any sort of preferential treatment.

- **In advance, online (for pick-up at a specific location).** This is your best bet: the rates are far better (even if you order from a currency exchange that has a high street or airport presence too). Some currency exchanges will even provide free delivery of your cash. Bear in mind that if you want to use this service, you'll need to pay with a debit card.

    - If you're in the UK, Money Saving Expert has a fantastic tool called TravelMoneyMax to help you compare rates across various online sellers: www.worktravel.co/max.

    - I don't *think* any other country has a comparison tool like TravelMoneyMax, so you'll need to do your own comparisons by Googling "order foreign currency" and clicking on some of the links that appear in the search results.

Extra tips:

- If you must buy currency before you set off, try to start looking into it as far in advance as possible: you can track the exchange rate daily and pounce as soon as the rates are in your favour.

- Remember that no two currency exchanges are equal: the rates could vary widely, even on the same street. Shop around for the best deal.

- Buying currency is counted as a cash withdrawal, so you could face some hefty fees if you buy currency using a credit card (just like you would if you used a credit card to withdraw money from an ATM).

Setting up a bank account in the destination country

If you're going to be staying in one country for a significant length of time, you could also think about opening a bank account there and using TransferWise to transfer money to it (see **Chapter 5: Freelance From Anywhere** for more information). That way, you'll avoid all those nasty transaction fees. Not all countries/banks allow it if you're not a resident in that country, but it's worth looking into. Google "opening a bank account [name of country]" for relevant articles on the subject, or ask a question in the Nomad Forum (www.worktravel.co/nomadforum).

What do we do?

The best option for you will depend on your situation, preferences and ability to deal with hassle. Just in case you're interested though, here's what we do. (On the "ability to deal with hassle" spectrum, I place us at "able to deal with a bit of hassle in order to avoid significant fees, but unwilling to spend hours and hours trying to recover every last cent.)

Whenever we're in Europe, we use our MetroBank (www.worktravel.co/metrobank) credit and debit cards. MetroBank is a UK-based bank, and there are no fees on purchases or withdrawals anywhere in Europe.

We also make sure we always have cash on us: many stores (including supermarkets) don't accept credit or debit cards.

In the USA, we were able to open a bank account with Bank of America – which enables us to make fee-free withdrawals (from Bank of America ATMs) and purchases. Our MetroBank cards would charge us 1.9% for both, plus a £1 ATM fee – which isn't extortionate compared to what other banks charge, but we're often in the States for a couple of months at a time so we thought it was worth opening an account there.

We found it relatively easy to open our BoA account, but we did it quite a while ago and we've heard they're a lot stricter these days when it comes to opening accounts for foreigners.

Elsewhere in the world... we tend to just use our MetroBank cards and take the hit. We don't like all the fees associated with prepaid travel cards, and we don't like the idea of buying currency before we set off for somewhere new: even if we get the world's best exchange rate, we'd rather not have a lot of cash on us.

One thing we NEVER do – wherever we are – is withdraw money using our credit cards. And we always try to suss out the ATMs where there isn't an extra "ATM operator" fee.

Calculating your cost of living

We've been calculating our monthly expenses for well over two years now – mainly out of interest, but also because it ensures we don't go overboard on needless purchases (because we'd have to record it later that evening and feel bad about ourselves).

Here's how you can do it too (based on what we do):

1: Use The Birdy every day to record your day's expenses

With The Birdy (www.worktravel.co/birdy), you reply to a daily email listing everything you spent that day – and you can use a really clever hashtagging system to divide up your daily expenses into anything you like. A few of the hashtags we use (frequently) are #coffee, #groceries, #transport, #mealsout. You can then go into The Birdy dashboard and view pie charts depicting your spending habits.

Barcelona last year was the first time we spent more on wine than we did on coffee. In Chiang Mai, the #massages hashtag gets used way more than #groceries (we mainly eat street food when we're there). And in London, #takeaway makes a fair few appearances – as does #health (because we do all our dentist/doctor/optician stuff when we're there).

Note: the currency that you use in The Birdy has to remain consistent – which means that if you set it up in dollars and you're currently living in Spain, you'll need to convert your euros to dollars first.

2: Incorporate your flights

Divide the cost of the flight between all the months that you'll be staying in the place that you flew to.

(For tips on getting the best-value flights, read the **bonus chapter: Travel Like A Pro** at the end of this book.)

3: That's it!

At the end of each month, look through and see where your money's gone.

You could then use that information to figure out what your spending priorities are (meals out? wine? exercise classes?), and use Numbeo's "cost of living" tool (www.worktravel.co/numbeo) to see how much those things would cost in other cities – and therefore whether those cities would suit your budget requirements.

There are a few other apps that do the same as The Birdy – Trail Wallet for iPhone and iPad (www.worktravel.co/trailwallet) gets good reviews, for example.

Paying taxes as a digital nomad

The topic of tax is a tricky one for digital nomads – and it's something we get asked about a lot because no one *quite* knows how we're meant to go about reporting or paying tax correctly.

If you spend barely any time in your "home" country, should you pay your taxes there? Should you pay any taxes to a different country if you sell an ebook while you're in Thailand that you wrote while you were in six other countries? Or what about if you agree to do a project for a client while you're in Spain, work on it on a plane while you cross the airspace of nine other countries, and get helped by your virtual assistant in India?

I can't offer any specific advice on any of this, I'm afraid! At first I thought I could: I assumed I'd be able to offer generic-yet-helpful-enough advice based on what *we* do with our own tax affairs. But after doing extensive research into the matter, I've concluded that any advice I give will probably be useless to everyone: there's no such thing as generic-yet-helpful-enough advice when it comes to tax, *especially* for people who travel while they work!

So instead, I'm going to point you in the direction of some useful resources. All of them assume that you want to know how to go about paying tax legally rather than how to avoid it.

- **Nomad Forum** (www.worktravel.co/nomadforum) is filled to the brim with fantastic advice, expertise and personal accounts when it comes to tax. Just type in "tax" in the search box to see all manner of Q&As, or "tax [country where you're from]" if you'd like to see more specific search results.

- **Greenback Expat Tax Services** (www.worktravel.co/greenback) is aimed specifically for Americans living abroad, and it comes highly recommended by many digital nomads.

- **Small Business Bodyguard** (www.worktravel.co/bodyguard) was created by business lawyer and intellectual property strategist Rachel Rogers. It's a resource containing documents, step-by-step instructions, a membership site, checklists, plug 'n' play policies and more for people who are starting up their own business. Before you buy the resource, you can download a "lawyer-approved, quick and dirty legal checklist for your small business" for free. SBB is mainly for Americans (or people setting up their business in the States).

- **Flag Theory** (www.worktravel.co/flag) is – according to the website – "a framework for strategically planting 'flags' (such as a bank account, legal entity, or property) in different countries and jurisdictions". The idea is that by doing so, you're able to increase your freedom, reclaim your privacy, and legally decrease the tax you have to pay. While you may not necessarily support every aspect of flag theory, the website does a good job of explaining your options when it comes to tax. This article is a useful starting point: www.worktravel.co/

flagnomad.

- **Foreign Earned Income Exclusion** (www.worktravel.co/irs) is a page from the IRS website which provides information for US citizens and US resident aliens who live abroad. While you're taxed on your worldwide income by default, you may qualify for an exclusion (up to a certain amount of your foreign earnings).

Whatever you decide to do, consider hiring an accountant: they'll remove all the burden of working out what you're meant to be filing and when, and they'll also be able to guide you as to what expenses you can and can't claim.

You should also keep track of the following at all times:

- Your income (how much, when and where it was generated)

- Any expenses that are business-related and can offset business income

- The number of days you spend in a particular country/outside your "home" country during the tax year (your length of stay somewhere can have an impact on your tax-filing requirements – especially if you're American)

Conclusion

It's tricky to cover money and taxes in any amount of detail because the advice is so specific to each individual situation. Where you're from, where you're living, how quickly you move around, how you make money, and your tolerance for hassle are all important factors in determining how you should manage your finances.

While this chapter has been a bit of a grab-bag of links, I hope you can understand why – and I also hope it's provided you with a good starting point for doing further research.

Chapter 3: Guard Your Data

Rob and I actually wrote a book called Protect Your Tech (www.worktravel.co/protectyourtech), and it covers everything you need to know about keeping your data and gadgets safe – whether you're a digital nomad or not.

In this chapter, I've repeated some of the information that's most relevant and most important to people who travel while they work. So yes – if you already own Protect Your Tech, you'll notice a bit of duplication. But if you don't own it and you find this chapter interesting, you'll find lots more detail on many more subjects in there.

When it comes to digital security, the main difference between people who work in an office and people who travel while they work is: WIFI. You're likely to spend your time connecting to a number of wifi networks as you work from cafes, airports, open city wifi networks and so on – exposing your data to opportunistic nasties as you do so.

Luckily, ensuring the security of your data doesn't need to be at all difficult. In fact, just installing two small pieces of software will make you so secure that hackers will pass you over in search of easier prey. Sounds good, huh?

Before I go on to explain what those two pieces of software are, I'll briefly explain just why they're so necessary if you travel while you work. (Feel free to skip ahead to "How to protect yourself" if you don't feel the need to know about the dangers in detail.)

The dangers

It's worth remembering that wifi is just a way to transmit data using radio waves – which means that when you type in your Facebook password (for example), it passes *through the air* to the router that sends it to Mr Zuckerberg's servers on your behalf. And while radio waves are miraculous things, what they're definitely *not* is secure: just like anyone can tune in and listen to police radio or air traffic control, a malicious person could do the same with your data.

Of course, some security measures have been built on top of wifi to make it more secure – but as I explain later, those measures are probably a lot less effective than you imagine they are.

There are specific dangers associated with two different types of wifi: open wifi networks, and password-protected public wifi.

Open wifi networks

An open network is one where you just click "connect" and

you're online – with no need for a password at all. You might even find that your smartphone connects to open networks automatically.

Open networks are obviously convenient, but if the network isn't protected by a password, there's nothing to stop anyone from joining it and monitoring all the data that passes through it: a process known as "sniffing". As data sent over wifi is unencrypted unless you specifically use a secure connection (which I come to later), it shows up to a hacker as plain text – so they can literally pull your passwords, personal data and the addresses of sites you visit out of the air.

When you're using an open public network, you should act as if everyone else in the vicinity is looking over your shoulder at everything you type and every site you visit. Which, in busier branches of Starbucks, they might just be doing anyway.

Password-protected public wifi

Because open wifi doesn't have much going for it in terms of security, it's common for public networks to be protected by a password. It might seem a bit pointless (a hacker could just buy a coffee and ask the barista for the password like anyone else), but there's actually a valuable security advantage to protecting a network with a password – even if many people know and use that password.

The advantage is that on a password-protected network, every user has their own individual connection to the access point, or router. This connection is encrypted (usually using a standard called WPA2), which means that anyone sniffing the data that passes through the air will just see a meaningless string of garbled data. The access point has the key that's needed to decrypt the data so it can pass your request on to the website you want to visit, but it's very difficult for anyone without the key to do so.

This means that if a hacker arrives once you're already connected to the network, they won't be able to steal your data because your connection is encrypted. If a hacker is already on the network when you arrive, however, they can eavesdrop on your initial connection to the access point – just like overhearing two people agreeing on a secret code word. By doing this they can learn the individual encryption key that's being used between you and the access point, and use it to decrypt all your traffic. At this point, your traffic can be monitored just as easily as if you were on a totally open network.

It's also easy for a hacker arriving later to kick you off the network (perhaps only for a second, so you don't even notice), allowing them to "overhear" and steal the key when your computer attempts to automatically reconnect.

It gets worse before it gets better…

You might think that you're safe if you arrive at the cafe already logged in to a service like Amazon (where your credit card details are stored) – because you won't actually have to "send" the password and allow a hacker to pluck it out of the air. Unfortunately that's not the case: websites use "session cookies" to track you as you move from page to page so that you don't have to keep re-entering your account details. So even if you arrive at the wifi hotspot already connected to Amazon, someone can intercept your session cookie and use it to access your account on their own computer with exactly the same access that you have (because as far as Amazon is concerned, they *are* you).

If you think this all sounds so utterly complicated that you'd have to be supremely unlucky to be sharing a cafe with a master hacker… nope. Just search YouTube for "hack WPA2 network", and prepare to be terrified when you see how many videos there are giving step-by-step instructions that need only a modicum of tech knowledge.

How to protect yourself

Now you're aware of the bad news: wifi is intrinsically insecure. Open networks are *really* insecure, but password-protected networks are only slightly better.

(Your "home" network is far more secure but definitely not impervious: hackers would first have to use password-cracking techniques to figure out your network password, and *then* they could use the techniques I mentioned in the previous section to steal your data.)

So what can you do about it? Luckily, there are a few simple steps you can take to vastly increase your online security…

Use HTTPS

Many websites offer access via HTTPS rather than HTTP – with the "S" standing for "secure". This basically means that the website creates a secure, encrypted tunnel (using a security protocol called SSL/TLS) between you and the site.

Unlike the encryption that's provided by the wireless network, this tunnel encrypts your traffic all the way from your computer to the website you want to visit – rather than just as far as the access point. This means that even if someone eavesdrops on your connection to the access point and cracks that code, there's *another* layer of encryption inside (like keeping a safe inside a locked room), which there's no way they can break.

What this means in practical terms is that if you can see "HTTPS" and a padlock symbol in your browser's address bar, the information that passes between you and the site will be safe. But although HTTPS is used as the default by many major sites (including Gmail, Facebook and Twitter), a lot of sites have both secure and non-secure versions – and even if you remember to start your visit by typing "HTTPS", you could easily click a link that sends you back to the non-secure HTTP version without noticing.

To avoid having to worry about this, you can use a browser extension for Chrome and Firefox called HTTPS Everywhere (www.worktravel.co/httpseverywhere). The extension is simple, but effective: all it does is automatically re-route you to the HTTPS version of a website when one is available.

HTTPS Everywhere operates in the background automatically,

so you don't have to do anything – except double-check that you can see "HTTPS" and the padlock symbol in your browser before before entering any particularly sensitive information like credit card details.

It's important to realise that HTTPS Everywhere only *activates* the secure versions of websites that offer HTTPS security – it can't *make* a website secure if it isn't already. But as it's as easy as installing a browser plugin and forgetting about it, there's no reason not to.

So what about those sites that *don't* have a secure HTTPS version available? For those, you'll have to take another security measure: using a VPN.

Use a VPN

If you're going to spend a significant amount of time working from public wifi connections (whether password-protected or not), it's worth significantly levelling up your security by using a VPN (Virtual Private Network).

Mentioned briefly in **Chapter 1: Settle In Fast**, a VPN is a network of servers around the world. It creates a secure, encrypted tunnel between your computer and one of those servers, and – because your traffic is encrypted from your computer until it reaches the VPN server – there's no way that anyone sniffing your local network would be able to access your data.

For practical purposes, then, a VPN gives you the same benefits as a site that uses HTTPS – *but it does it whether the site has an HTTPS option available or not.* This is important, because by using a VPN you're no longer relying on a site you want to visit having an HTTPS option available: you're taking your security into your own hands, and you know that as long as your VPN is switched on, you're safe against anyone attempting to hack your wifi network.

(However, your best bet is to use a VPN *plus* HTTPS: if you only used a VPN, there's a small chance your data could be intercepted by someone hacking at the *website's* end rather than yours. As HTTPS Everywhere sorts out the HTTPS layer for you automatically anyway, there's no reason not to.)

Unlike just using HTTPS Everywhere, a small amount of effort is required: a VPN is often only effective if you remember to switch it on, so you should get into the habit of enabling it as soon as you sit down in a cafe or anywhere other than your home network. And you should always be vigilant, because you can get disconnected from the VPN for one reason or another without you noticing – meaning your traffic goes back to passing non-securely through the local network.

There *are* free VPN services available, but they're often slow and will limit the amount of time you can spend on them. If you're regularly working on the move, paying for a VPN service is a small investment for a great solution.

As I said in **Chapter 1: Settle In**, my recommended VPN is TorGuard (www.worktravel.co/torguard). We've tried out an awful lot of VPNs over the years, and this is by far our favourite.

It costs $9.99 a month (or $29.99 for six months paid upfront), and this is why we love it:

- It's way faster than the free VPNs: you won't have to amuse yourself 50 times a minute while your TV show buffers.

- It allows up to five connections per account – which means you can install it on your computer, your partner's computer, both your smartphones and your iPad.

- It always seems to work perfectly. (We've used so many services in the past – even paid ones – where the service fails to connect, or drops out halfway through.)

- It has servers in about 40 countries, which means you'll be able to watch TV shows online from countries as wide-ranging as the UK, USA, Canada, Australia, Egypt, Germany, Mexico, Moldova, Latvia and India.

- The customer service is excellent.

Really, using a VPN alongside HTTPS Everywhere is all you need to keep yourself safe against most of the threats you're likely to encounter. There are lots of other services to help you remain *anonymous*, but they're not connected with your safety so I won't go into them here.

Use different passwords for everything

Let's say you forgot to switch on the VPN, and someone

manages to intercept your connection as you're logging in to a "non-HTTPS" website. Even if that website stores absolutely no personal information and no credit card numbers, the hacker still has your username (usually your email address) and password. They can then try out that username and password on all other sites too – including ones that *do* have sensitive information about you.

And that's why you need different passwords for everything. The problem with having multiple passwords, though, is that it's hard to remember them all.

Enter... the online password manager. There are a few different password managers around, but our favourite one by far is LastPass (www.worktravel.co/lastpass). It's basically your very cool alternative to pure memory. It sits as a little extension on your browser, and it stores all your usernames and passwords in its online "vault". You just need to remember ONE password – your "master password" for logging in to LastPass – in order to access all your other usernames and passwords.

Whenever you need to log in to anything, you won't need to remember your password: LastPass is ready and waiting to autocomplete the username/email and password fields for you.

You can install LastPass on as many of your devices as you like, which means you can easily log in to all your websites through your phone, computer, tablet and so on. (You'll need to pay $12 a year to have it installed on your smartphone.)

There's a brilliant extra benefit for businesses too (also

mentioned in **Chapter 7: Run The Best Biz**): if you need to share access to a particular site with a friend, colleague or freelancer, LastPass will allow you to give them your login credentials *without revealing what they are* – and you can revoke access at any time.

Conclusion

To summarise: wifi isn't at all secure. The good news is that there are some easy ways to protect yourself against the local hacking attempts that you're at risk of when you use public wifi.

Combining use of a VPN with HTTPS Everywhere is a good balance of security and ease, but it doesn't mean you can relax: you should still do quick manual checks before entering sensitive information to make sure you haven't, for example, been disconnected from your VPN without noticing. If you can see the padlock symbol and the "HTTPS" in your browser bar, you know you're safe.

Note: this chapter has given you the digital nomad essentials, but for the full lowdown, check out our dedicated book: **Protect Your Tech** *(www.worktravel.co/protectyourtech). It contains more information on protecting your data, plus chapters on securing your email, using the right passwords, shopping and socialising safely, protecting your laptop (and knowing what to do if it goes missing), keeping the contents of your phone safe, and securing all the files you have stored in the cloud.*

Chapter 4: Be A Productivity Powerhouse

Oh hi there, can of worms!

The topic of "productivity while travelling" is a borderline obsession of ours – but we're not the only ones. Almost every digital nomad/"escape the office" blog has tips, hacks, apps, strategies, ideas and pleas for advice when it comes to being both mobile and productive – and it's not hard to understand why.

None of us are regular employees: we can't just rock up at an office, sit around all day doing the bare minimum, go home and get paid.

- As business owners and freelancers, we have to do the work (and work on the *right* things) if we're to earn money.

- As remote workers, we have more to prove to our

employers: they don't know what we're up to all day every day, so we have to show we're worth our salary though the results we create for the company.

At the same time, we don't want to be constantly working our butts off if we can help it: we want to go out and experience whichever city we're living in.

And that problematic little contradiction – needing to work, but wanting (and being able) to play – can be our undoing. There's just too much to do, see, eat and take in. And what's the point in living this lifestyle if we rarely step foot outside the darn apartment?

It's a tricky one.

Rob and I found ourselves in a perhaps unusual psychological situation when we first started travelling and setting up a business: we doubled down on the work – *work that didn't even matter* – because we panicked ourselves into thinking that if we stopped, our business would never get off the ground. We left fun and life experience by the wayside in order to work like crazy people on things that essentially made no difference to our business success.

Most other people we've come across have the opposite experience: they find it hard to get into the groove of work because they want to get out there and have fun.

Neither situation is great, but we've figured out some guidelines that allow for a happy medium. It's all down to these four things:

- Have a routine
- Filter out distractions
- Set up an optimal working environment
- Outsource

Here goes!

Have a routine

We're all in the enviable position of having no routines set upon us. (If you're a remote worker, that may be less true – but you still probably have more flexibility in your working day than the average employee sitting in an office.)

But for all its freedoms and benefits (going to a movie in the middle of the afternoon; avoiding rush hour on the train…), it's potentially ruinous for certain aspects of our lives – "getting work done" being one of them.

Most of the successful digital nomads we know have a firmly fixed daily routine. It may seem strange at first – after all, these people have escaped structure; they can do whatever they want, whenever they want! Why on earth would they impose on themselves something they've just liberated themselves from?

Because without routine, you wake up and don't quite know what to do with your day: it stretches out before you like a terrifyingly long, blank canvas. So you get up, you watch some TV, you make some breakfast, you remember you're out of milk, you go buy some milk, you think about what work to be getting on with... and before you know it it's halfway through the afternoon and your friends are all making plans to meet up for drinks later. So – seeing as you're going out soon anyway – you wash some plates, call your parents and then head out for beer. Or bulletproof coffee. Or water with a splash of lemon. Or whatever's fashionable among digital nomads at the moment.

Or – if you're anything like we used to be – you wake up and your entire day involves work. There's no cut-off point, so you just work work work – allowing tasks to drag on because there's no end point when you *must* finish. It takes far longer to get something done and dusted because you're just filling up all the time you have. And you don't get to fully experience or enjoy your city because you only go out to buy food or stretch your legs.

Both of these examples are at fairly extreme ends of the spectrum. But the general gist is this: if you don't have a routine, you don't know when you're meant to be working. If you adore work or worry about it, there's a good chance you'll do nothing else (so what's the point in travelling?). And if you love seeing the world and being out and about, you might find yourself choosing *not* to work most of the time – especially if you're in the initial stages and aren't noticing any traction from your efforts yet.

Routine gives you boundaries and expectations. For us, we know that we're meant to *finish* work by 3pm – which means we have to work fast and smart if we're to meet our daily deadline. We can't waste time on work of the "grazing" kind – stuff that makes no difference to our success. We *have* to figure out which tasks will have the biggest impact on our business and spend time on those instead.

For you, it might be the opposite: your routine might all be about making sure you get *started* by a certain time.

Our routine

A routine needs to be realistic if it's going to work in the long-term.

Here's what we do:

6am: Wake up, brush teeth and do exercise (I usually go outside and Rob stays in to do workout videos).

7.30am: Get in from walk (me), shower, make coffee, have a chat.

8am-12.30pm: Work (breakfast happens in there somewhere, while working).

12.30pm-3pm: Work at a cafe of some sort for a change of scenery.

3pm: Lunch.

The rest of the afternoon and evening: See friends, see the sights, go on little excursions, go out for drinks, have dinner, whatever we like. If we have a lot of work to do, we'll do some of it after lunch and *then* go out to have fun (but we always give ourselves a deadline, like "Work DEFINITELY stops at 5pm").

11-11.30pm: Bed!

—

This routine works really well for us. It's essentially about getting exercise out the way first (see **Chapter 1: Settle In Fast** for exercise ideas), then getting down to work at a time when we know we're at our most productive and creative.

Sometimes we mix up the routine a bit: we might go out in the morning and do work later in the day. For the most part though, this is what we stick to every day, six days a week. (On a Sunday, we still get up at 6am but we try to keep to the rule of "No. Work. Whatsoever.")

This routine isn't meant to be a blueprint or anything! It's just to show you what *we* do. If you want to sleep until noon, go out with friends and *then* work from 6pm until midnight, that's fine: just make sure you commit to it.

If you want to see some more examples of daily routines, head to the **Appendix** for interviews with other digital nomads.

Resources to help with your routine

Here's a selection of books, websites and tools that might inspire you to develop your own routine and good working habits:

- The Tiny Habits Method (website and free course): www.worktravel.co/tinyhabits

- Coach Me (app that helps you reach your goals): www.worktravel.co/coach

- Mini Habits: Smaller Habits, Bigger Results (book by Stephen Guise): www.worktravel.co/minihabits

- The Checklist Manifesto: How to Get Things Right (book by Atul Gawande): www.worktravel.co/checklist

- There are some fantastic answers on Quora to the question "What are the best daily routines of highly productive people?": www.worktravel.co/quora

- The Quora answers to the question "What are the best ways for non 9-5 types to build structure and social interaction into their daily routines?" are also pretty good: www.worktravel.co/quora2

Stay focused and filter out distractions

Everyone has different kinds of distractions, and different ways of dealing with them. Rather than try to guess what yours are, here's a list of web apps, online tools and strategies we use – which you can pick and choose from if any of them look appealing.

- **Do your most important task before checking your**

emails. I'll be the first to admit: I don't and *can't* do this. I check my emails while putting my contact lenses in and brushing my teeth in the morning. But Rob has this down to a fine art, and it really does help him stay focused in the morning: it means other people's priorities don't get in the way of *his* #1 priority – whether it's writing a book, recording a podcast, planning a webinar or mapping out a business process.

- **Prevent distracting and non-urgent emails from entering your inbox.**

    1. Unsubscribe from EVERY mailing list you find yourself on but never read. This is easier done than said! All you have to do is visit Unroll Me (www.worktravel.co/unroll) and they can handle it all for you.

    2. Sign up for new lists using the Gmail "plus sign" trick (more here: www.worktravel.co/plustrick). Then filter anything sent to that address to skip the inbox, get marked as "read", and be given a "mailing list" label so you can schedule a specific time to read them.

- **Spend 15 minutes each evening planning out the following day.** This is what we do, and it's fantastic for keeping us on track and making sure we don't lose focus.

    We use Trello (www.worktravel.co/trello) to do all our

planning.

- **Embrace the Pomodoro Technique.** This one is huge for Rob. He used to do at least 12 hours of low-intensity screen time each day, conning himself into thinking he was crazy busy. Now, with the Pomodoro Technique (www.worktravel.co/pomodoro), he spends 25 minutes on a set task with absolutely no distractions. The amount he can get done in an hour is – in his words – "terrifying".

    By scheduling six pomodoros of activity the previous day (which can include one pomodoro for responding to emails), he knows that even if he only gets three hours of work done, he'll still do enough to move all his important projects forward.

    The Pomodoro Technique isn't for everyone because it's quite intense. I use it only when there are certain tasks that I know I'll otherwise ponder and procrastinate and take too long over: it ensures I get it done in 25 minutes rather than two hours.

    If you like the idea of using a dedicated "Pomodoro timer", there are plenty available – like Pomodoto (www.worktravel.co/pomodoto), which is free and can be downloaded for Mac, Windows, Android and iOS, and is also available as a Chrome extension.

- **Batch your "meetings" (phone call meetings).** This never goes as well as it should for us, but we aim to compress all meetings and calls into one or two mornings or afternoons a week. Preparing for phone calls and then getting back into work/creativity mode can be time-consuming, so for us it's easier to get them all out of the way in one go.

Useful web app alert! With appointment-booking software You Can Book Me (www.worktravel.co/bookme), you can set the dates and times that you're available each week, then send a special link to anyone who wants to book a meeting or phone call with you.

- **Track what you've achieved.** We use iDoneThis (www.worktravel.co/donethis) to record what we've done every day. While we rarely look back at previous days, the act of writing it down each evening is useful – and it pushes us to make sure we *have* achieved something each day!

    You could also try AskMeEvery (www.worktravel.co/askme): it emails you every day asking a simple yes/no for specific activities – e.g. "Did I exercise today?"

- **Get a good pair of earphones if the noise of neighbours, traffic or fellow cafe-dwellers is driving you nuts.** These ones by Kransen come highly recommended: they're tiny, they don't get tangled up, *and* they come with a built-in microphone (useful for calls): www.worktravel.co/kransen.

- **Consider coworking spaces** – especially if you struggle to concentrate in cafes but still want to get out of the apartment and around other people. The atmosphere is usually much quieter, and you might find it more motivating because everyone around you is also working. There are a number of coworking directories online, like ShareDesk (www.worktravel.co/sharedesk). Alternatively, do a Google search for "coworking [name of city]".

- **Make use of music/sounds designed to help you concentrate.** For example:

    - Coffitivity (www.worktravel.co/coffitivity), a free web and phone app that "recreates the ambient sounds of a cafe to boost your creativity and help you work better".

    - Focus@Will (www.worktravel.co/focus), which contains "music scientifically optimized to boost concentration and focus" in an app on your web browser and phone. It's free for 30 days, then about $6 per month after that.

    - You can also find lots of free "concentration music" playlists on YouTube and Spotify.

Set up a great working environment

When we lived permanently in London and worked regular

jobs, Rob had a massive corner desk in our living room. He only really used it when required to do extra work outside of office hours, but he still made sure it was set up perfectly for his needs. There was the black Herman Miller-esque chair whose height I was banned from adjusting, the Anglepoise-esque lamp that mustn't be swivelled, the immaculately arranged drawers and filing system, and the different wires and cables Blu-Tacked to the desk so that they wouldn't go AWOL.

It wasn't just the desk that made his working environment perfect – there was also the internet. We had fibre-optic broadband installed (and TBH it still blows our minds when we're back in the apartment: we can download a movie in the time it takes me to read the IMDB synopsis and realise I don't want to watch it anymore).

As you might imagine, it was a bit of an adjustment when we started to travel while working. Not only was Rob's perfect desk setup gone, but sometimes he didn't even have a table to work from. And parting ways with our internet connection would have been easier if the internet in other places at least *worked* in some sense – but occasionally our apartments were without wifi for days.

Rather than give up or search for some sort of holy grail of productive working environment, we decided to find some workarounds to our issues. At the same time, we tried hard to loosen up and stop acting as if the world had ended every time we saw the "This webpage is not available" message.

In the next couple of sections I run through some of the ways we've managed to optimise our workspace and stay as productive as we can.

Optimise your workspace

- Before you book an apartment, take a look at the space and imagine yourself living there. Is there a spot where you imagine you'll be comfortable working? And be honest with yourself: if there's absolutely no table space and you can't bear working from bed, will you be able to be productive while you're there – or alternatively, are you willing and able to find a wifi cafe or coworking space for all the hours you need to work?

- Do you work best with a mouse or any other additional bits of hardware? Find a way to make room for them in your carry-on if you do, or else buy them when you arrive. There are some excellent travel-sized options available, like these:

    - If you normally like to have your computer screen at eye level, the Roost laptop stand is lightweight and easy to use: www.worktravel.co/roost.

    - If you use the Roost (or any other laptop stand) and need an external keyboard, there's a huge range of portable keyboards on Amazon – including foldable ones and ones which roll up: www.worktravel.co/keyboard.

- Do you usually use a mouse? There are plenty of tiny, wireless options on the market. Many of them use Bluetooth, but if you'd prefer more battery life for your buck, there are also mice that have tiny "receivers" which you plug into a USB port of your laptop. Like this amazing mini-mouse (which has an 18-month battery life): www.worktravel.co/mouse.

- Would you love to have a standing desk? There *are* some portable standing desks available – like the ZestDesk (www.worktravel.co/zestdesk) and StandStand (www.worktravel.co/standstand). They'll still take up a lot of space in your baggage though, so it depends what your priorities are. The other alternative is to do what Rob always does: find a cardboard box or stack of books, and place it on top of another surface like a chest of drawers, table or even bed.

- If your laptop lacks a decent set of speakers and you're fussy about that sort of thing, some of today's travel speakers offer incredible quality in tiny little packages. We no longer have a travel speaker (we just use regular ol' laptop speakers), but we've heard amazing things about this the Kinivo ZX100 – which works with almost all phones, laptops and tablets: www.worktravel.co/zx100.

Deal with wifi issues

Ah yes, wifi. (In my head, that's "argh yes, wifi".) When it's working fine, we take it for granted. When it's playing up, however, we get in a panic, hurl all manner of abusive words in its direction, and bemoan how technology can still be so crap in this day and age.

Below are some ways to deal with wifi issues in your apartment. They're not technological solutions – you'll need an expert for that – but simple preventative measures or backup solutions that have worked for us.

- Simple one, this: before you book somewhere to rent, figure out how good the wifi is. What do reviewers say about it, for example? If you're staying in an Airbnb apartment, you can also **ask the host to do a speed test for you** – send them here: www.worktravel.co/speedtest.

- Buy a **prepaid SIM that you can tether** – to use as a backup if the wifi in your apartment is playing up. (Read **Chapter 1: Settle In Fast** for more information on how to find the best SIM card for where you're living.)

- Consider buying a **mobile wifi hotspot**, which is a little wireless device that allows multiple users to share a single 3G or 4G data connection via their laptops, tablets and phones. It's basically your own personal wifi network that you can take with you wherever you go.

    All you need to do is buy an "unlocked" device, then get

a prepaid or pay-as-you-go SIM card in the country in which you're living. The SIM card needs to allow tethering (so that the internet connection can be shared between the device and your computer/s) for it to work.

While a mobile wifi hotspot isn't free (and the internet speed won't be as fast as really good wifi), it's a great backup to have available.

We have the sexily named Huawei E5330 mobile hotspot (www.worktravel.co/hotspot), because it does three things in one: not only is it a mobile hotspot, but it also acts as a wifi extender (useful if you're in a large apartment and the router is at one end of it) aaaand it allows you to connect more than one device when you only have one username and passport (e.g. in a hotel room).

- **Get a Didlogic number.** This is covered in more detail in **Chapter 5: Freelance From Anywhere.** Didlogic (www.worktravel.co/didlogic) is *great* if you have people needing to phone you but Skype isn't working due to dodgy wifi. Here's how it works:

    - You buy a local SIM card for whichever country you're in, and then you buy a Didlogic number through the website (the cost of which varies, but it's in the region of $0.70 a month) that forwards to that local number very inexpensively.

    - You can choose a Didlogic number that's based in

any country and get it forwarded to any local SIM for a tiny cost.

- The upshot is that anyone who needs to call you can dial a local number and talk to you as if it were a regular, local phone call. The cost to them will be the price of a local phone call, and it won't cost much more for you. What's more, there's no internet involved.

• Get Skype To Go (www.worktravel.co/skypetogo). Again, this is covered in more detail in **Chapter 5: Freelance From Anywhere**. Unlike Didlogic, it's more useful if you want to be the one making phone calls to people in other countries, but you can't do it through "regular" Skype because your internet connection is sucky. It gives you numbers that let you call anyone abroad from any mobile or landline while avoiding international calling charges... *and* avoiding the internet.

• If you're a regular user of Google Docs and Sheets, **enable the "offline" option** so that you can continue to work while your internet is playing up. There are instructions on how to do it here: www.worktravel.co/docsoffline.

Outsource

If there's one life skill I wish I'd learnt earlier, it would be hiring other people to help me with my work. In fact, I wish I'd done it right at the start – even though back then, I was far less busy and could easily do all the work myself. Why? Because at least I'd have had the time to learn how to hire and how to manage people, and it would have prepared me for times when I *didn't* have the time but desperately needed the help.

There's also the fact that I'm just no good at lots of things, and it's far better to get someone else to do them – someone who has experience and skills in the task.

If you're currently trying to do everything yourself, give some thought to what can easily be given to someone else. It might include:

- Admin work that anyone with a set of instructions could follow and implement

- Design/development/writing/sales/marketing/PR work that you don't have the skills for

- Work that you *could* do yourself but would be better off passing on to a specialist who can do it faster and better – leaving you to focus on what you're best at

- Accounting and bookkeeping for your business

- A whole range of other things – including your inbox!

Many people struggle to pass responsibility over to someone else, but it's particularly difficult for digital nomads. We can't meet potential candidates and assess them in person, we can't have office banter with them and build up a rapport, we don't know how hard they're working because we're not sitting in a physical office with them, and our timezone changes frequently – making it difficult for regular "catch up" meetings.

There are actually some huge benefits to these perceived setbacks, and it's not that difficult to hire and manage a remote worker or remote team once you get into it! In the next couple of chapters I cover some resources and strategies for hiring and managing people who you might never meet in person.

Conclusion

Some friends and I were discussing routines and working habits recently. (Yes: they were also digital nomads. No normal person would spend a night in a bar debating the merits of the Pomodoro Technique.)

One said, "I work REALLY hard between 9am and 2pm, because that's when I work best. After that, there's zero point in trying to make myself work, because I'll barely get anything done."

I think the secret of being productive is figuring out what times of day you work best, and then making sure you free up those hours every day. Tools and techniques to filter out distractions and optimise your workspace can be extremely useful – but they'll only help if you're in the mood to work already.

Chapter 5: Freelance From Anywhere

Lots of people begin their digital nomad journey by freelancing. Either they're freelancers already and decide to make a leap and do it from anywhere, or they quit their jobs, find a client or two, and start working while they travel.

It makes sense to start here: freelancing is usually the quickest and easiest route to making money if you can provide a service that people are willing to pay for. Rather than build up a business or throw time and cash into creating a product while you're concurrently trying to get to grips with perpetual travel, freelancing enables you to just find a few clients who are willing to pay you, then do work for them from wherever you happen to be. And by moving somewhere cheap when starting out (like South East Asia or even some parts of Europe), you give yourself a bit more "runway": your money lasts longer, so you have more time to figure out how to make a sustainable income and what sort of work/lifestyle combination satisfies you.

Freelancing is how we started out – with our copywriting business Mortified Cow. And even though we now run a business, we still do a bit of copywriting work on the side because we enjoy it and it pays well.

Freelancing isn't *completely* plain-sailing though – at least not at first. In this chapter I cover some of the things we learnt along the way – things we'd have really appreciated knowing at the start!

First though, a quick general note about the chapter: I've tried to focus solely on what you as a freelancer *who travels* will need to know and consider. I haven't included any information that's relevant to *all* freelancers – like finding clients or deciding what to charge.

Some principles of freelancing while you travel

Want a happy freelancer-client relationship? Here are some principles that may help you get one.

The right clients don't mind

If you've got clients who are a bit iffy about Skype calls and constantly enquire as to when you'll be back for a face-to-face meeting, you won't be able to change their attitude enough for you both to be satisfied with the end result. They'll *always* think the job is inferior because you're not in the same country as them, which means you won't get the referrals you deserve – and your clients will never be a dream to work for.

There are plenty of people who won't mind in the slightest that you work from around the world. In fact, many of our clients love the fact that we're not stuck in an office trying to brainstorm with fellow cubicle dwellers whose only inspiration comes from the magical properties of an after-work pint.

When we first started getting referrals, our prospective clients would often ask for in-person meetings or worry about how things worked. So here's what we did: we thanked them for getting in touch, did an incy bit of background research into their business/company (so as to personalise the reply a bit more), then sent them a PDF document called "Pleased to meet moo". (The name of this document *only just about* made sense because our company is called Mortified Cow. Please don't think it's a term used frequently in copywriting circles or anything.)

The contents of the "Pleased to meet moo" document mentioned a few things about our business and the way we work, and – importantly – it also stated our "conditions": we work while we travel the world, which means we don't do in-person meetings, most correspondence happens over email, and phone calls necessarily take place over Skype (or Zoom – see later in this chapter).

This process stopped us all from wasting each other's time: they could make a decision straight away as to whether they were comfortable working with people they'd likely never meet in person.

> **Want to read and steal bits from our "Pleased to meet moo" document? Register your purchase of this book at www.worktravel.co to download the PDF!**

To clarify...

The right clients don't mind... as long as you put their needs first.

NEVER schedule a meeting using your timezone rather than theirs.

NEVER use delayed flights or Delhi Belly as an excuse for being late with work.

NEVER say the wifi hotspot at your Bali beach isn't up to scratch, so is it OK to call them when you're back at the apartment?

Those things are our problems as digital nomads, and our clients don't want to think that our lifestyles are leading to inferior delayed work.

Never respond to a client's email straight away

Because if you get them used to it, the moment you *don't* there's the risk that they'll think "Oh, they must be on a plane or something. Gee this sucks. I wouldn't have this problem if I were working with someone who wasn't a digital nomad."

The key is to be consistent. We commit to responding within a maximum of 24 hours, but we always try to delay responding by at least an hour – even if we're sitting at our laptops and working on that particular client's project at that moment.

(If you want to reply right away just to declutter your inbox, use the "send later" feature of Boomerang – a Gmail extension: www.worktravel.co/boomerang. You push "send" but the email doesn't get delivered until a time and date that you specify. It's free for up to ten emails a month; after that it's $4.99 a month. There's also another – more feature-heavy – extension called Mixmax – www.worktravel.co/mixmax. I discuss that in more detail later.)

It's not just about the digital nomad factor, of course; it's also that you shouldn't be at your client's beck and call *anyway*. It creates massive expectations on the part of the client, and soon you might find you're spending far too much time responding to their every email (which become more and more frequent) than actually doing the work.

You can only "train" clients in your methods up to a point

In my old job, non-tech-savvy clients would literally mail CDs of photos over to the office because they didn't know how to send such large files any other way.

And they'd print and sign their agreements with the company, and post them to us.

We don't have the luxury of a mailbox. (And actually, we'd hate to do things that way anyway.) So everything has to be done online. There are two ways of doing things online: the fast way and the slow way. Sometimes our clients are more comfortable with the slow way...

For document-signing we've tried *extremely hard* to insist on HelloSign (www.worktravel.co/hellosign – a cloud-based online signature tool which I discuss in more detail later). But some clients are having none of it. So they print out a document, sign it, then either take a photo or scan and email it back to us.

For photos and images... it's a process. We try asking for Dropbox-sharing, Ge.tt uploading, YouSendIt, anything. But the vast majority of clients just can't figure out how to use any of them. So we'll often receive photos one by one over email instead.

But you know... these aren't really deal-breakers. If we have wonderful clients who appreciate our hard work, give us useful and timely feedback, and are generally a joy to work with, we're not going to get all ultimatumy on them just because their scanned-in signature is a bit blurry.

If this sort of email correspondence fills you with dread, you can always hire a virtual assistant (see **Chapter 6: Hire Like A Champ**) to help you out. For example, you could forward the one-by-one emails with attached photos to your assistant, who'd download them all and store them neatly in Dropbox.

Don't lower your prices - even if you're living somewhere cheap

If you've chosen to spend time in a cheap South East Asian or South American country, your money will go a lot further. That doesn't mean you should lower your prices for clients, however. Here are a few reasons why:

- The fact that you're living in a cheaper place has nothing to do with how much you charge. How much you charge is based on the value your service provides – and nothing more.

- What happens when you move somewhere more expensive? Your clients and customers don't care that you've moved from Saigon to Sydney and the price of a baguette has gone up tenfold. They're going to resent it if you increase your prices despite no discernible improvements in quality or service.

- By keeping your prices in line with the value you provide for Western customers and clients, you'll be able to make more money and move outside cheap countries (if you want to) when you're ready. If you're charging the kinds of prices that mean you can only survive in cheaper countries, you're no longer location-independent.

Plenty of people *do* lower their prices because they can afford to and they think it helps them win more business, but I've never been tempted and I'm glad I've stuck to my guns.

Getting paid as a digital nomad freelancer

Winning a client and completing the project is hard enough – so you really don't want to wrap up with a wrangle about payment methods, currencies and exchange rates.

The default option for getting paid as a digital nomad is PayPal: it's easy and it's ubiquitous, but it's not cheap. Especially, as I explain later, when multiple currencies are involved.

So is there an alternative? What method *should* you be using to get paid for your services? In this section I go through some of your options.

(Note: these options are mainly written with Americans and Europeans in mind, but many of them will still be relevant if you're from a different country.)

The old-school option: cheque/check

The US banking system can seem ludicrously archaic: the most efficient way of paying someone is often still deemed to be mailing a small piece of paper hundreds of miles. But a happy side effect of the continued American reliance on cheques (or "checks", if you insist) is that most major banks allow you to pay them in via your bank's mobile app just by taking a photograph.

This means that if you have a US bank account and you're being paid by an American client (but not currently in the US yourself), a cheque might not be an entirely unrealistic option: you could get it sent to a virtual address (see **Chapter 1: Settle In Fast)**, forwarded on to wherever in the world you are, then use the app to pay it in remotely. It seems insane, but if you're dealing with large accounts departments who won't use another payment method, it is at least an option.

If your bank account is in the UK, Barclays has recently become the first UK bank to offer the "pay in by app" service, and others may follow suit.

The simplest-but-somewhat-upsetting option: PayPal

PayPal (www.worktravel.co/paypal) provides payment processing services to help you accept money through your website or from your clients.

It's easy and flexible, but pricey. The standard fee is 2.9% of the transfer amount plus $0.30 (or £0.20 for a UK PayPal account, or the rough international equivalent elsewhere). And if the PayPal account of the seller is registered in a different country from yours, it's 3.9% rather than 2.9%.

That's the bad news – and it *is* bad, because that's a hefty amount to be giving away – but the upside is that the person paying you can use their PayPal balance, bank transfer or credit card so there's no excuse for not paying you. PayPal also integrates with just about every piece of invoicing software out there.

Given how easy it is, you might decide to just factor the costs into the fee you charge for your services and try *really hard* not to look at the column in your account which shows the fees that have been deducted.

However, there's another unpleasant twist if your PayPal account is denominated in a different currency from the one you're billing in…

When we do work for US clients, we quote our fees and allow them to pay in US dollars – because otherwise it's hard for them to work out how much they're paying us *and* makes it even more of a challenge for them to pay. As the dollar is pretty much the global currency, lots of other contractors do the same.

The challenge is that when a US dollar transfer is made into a PayPal account that's denominated in another currency, PayPal converts the payment into that currency *at a horrible exchange rate that bears no relation to reality*. Yes, you could set up a separate US dollar balance on any PayPal account, but you'll still get stuffed by that same nasty exchange rate whenever you convert the money back to your home currency – and on a recent invoice of ours for a few thousand dollars, the exchange rate left us worse off by $103.

You could just keep a balance in the denomination in which your client is based and use it whenever you need to pay for something that's charged in that currency, but it's not ideal: many of your main expenses (like flights and accommodation) probably can't be paid for using PayPal. And it'll make your tax accounting bloomin' complicated.

Another simple-but-upsetting option: Stripe

Stripe (www.worktravel.co/stripe) is a lot like PayPal, but it allows people to just pay you by credit card without needing to set up an account or anything. It needs a bit of tech knowhow to integrate, but it gives you a lot of flexibility in return.

The fees are very similar to PayPal.

The secret option: PayPal Business Payments

PayPal Business Payments is an option so good that it's impossible to find anything on their website about it: a flat fee of only $0.50 for any payment amount up to $10,000. For larger payments, this can add up to a *gigantic* difference.

However, even once you *do* track it down, it comes with a buttload of restrictions:

- You need a US-based PayPal account.

- It's only for payments in US dollars.

- The payer can't use their credit card to pay – only PayPal balance or bank transfer.

- It only works for payments up to $10,000 (which is a

pretty high ceiling, but it's a restriction nonetheless).

- You have to issue an invoice using software that supports PayPal Business Payments.

In other words, you can't just tell someone how much they owe you: you have to issue an invoice using a specific piece of software, and they can click the button to pay.

And is there a list of software anywhere that supports PayPal Business Payments? Of course not: the whole thing is like a limited trial that was set up years ago and someone forgot to cancel. It does definitely work with Freshbooks (who have written about it here: www.worktravel.co/freshbooks) and Harvest (who have written about it here: www.worktravel.co/harvest), but there may be others.

The wildly unpredictable option: wire transfer

A wire transfer eliminates the small piece of paper and the high percentage-based fee, but it does introduce a whole new set of variables which mean you can never be sure how much money you're actually going to receive. There's a fee for sending, often a fee for receiving, plus intermediaries who may or may not take a cut depending on the route your money takes. And even then, it can be several days before your payment arrives.

A wire transfer is initiated by the person sending the money through their bank – and depending on the bank in question it might need to be done in person or over the phone, but it can often be done online.

The benefit over PayPal is that even though the fees are unpredictable, they're unlikely to add up to more than PayPal's 2.9% (for larger invoices, at least). Also, for cross-currency payments you'll only be charged the *real* exchange rate (as long as your bank isn't up to anything sneaky, and you can check with them in advance) so you won't be clobbered with that fee too.

The downside is that not all banks allow international wire transfers, and the fact that there's a fee for the sender makes it both a hassle *and* a perceived expense for them (even if you tell them to deduct the transfer fee from the amount they send you).

The best option for cross-currency payments: TransferWise

TransferWise (www.worktravel.co/transferwise) is 100% solid amazing for any situation where a client needs to pay you in a different currency from their own. For example, if you're a European contractor who charges in euros and your client is in the US and holding US dollars, TransferWise is far cheaper than a wire transfer and not much more effort for the payer than using PayPal.

The basic concept (using euros and dollars as an example) is:

- The client visits the TransferWise website, says how

many euros they want to send, and uploads the equivalent amount in US dollars from their debit card or bank account.

- TransferWise matches the transaction with one going in the other direction to save on conversion fees.

- The euros are deposited in your bank account a couple of days later.

The fee varies depending on the currency pairing, but can be as low as 0.5%. When the payer is setting up the transfer it clearly states what the fees are, when the money will arrive in the payee's account, and how much cheaper it is than a typical wire transfer – which can easily be more than $50.

If you sign up (or get your client to sign up) to TransferWise using our link, there are NO fees on the first transfer: www.worktravel.co/transferwise.

To summarise...

Clearly there's no perfect option, but the situation could probably be summed up as:

- If you qualify and don't mind the restrictions, use PayPal Business Payments.

- To keep things simple, take a deep breath and use PayPal (or Stripe).

- For cross-currency payments, use TransferWise. (Similar

services are coming onto the market, but nothing yet offers a comparable service or rates.)

- Avoid wire transfers if at all possible because they're so unpredictable and annoying to set up.

- Receiving a cheque/check isn't ideal, but is possible if your bank has an app that allows you to pay it in remotely.

The most important thing is to *discuss the payment methods you accept with your client before the job starts.* We've made the mistake of not doing this in the past, and it leaves a bad taste for everyone when a great project is rounded off with a week of ping-pong emails about how you should get paid.

Dealing with logistics (phone calls, paperwork, etc.)

Most of your correspondence with clients will probably take place over email, but from time to time you'll want to jump on a phone call or share a screen with them. Here's a mix-and-match collection of the tools you can use to make that happen more seamlessly while you live across timezones.

Note: if you're a remote worker (and you're either working for a distributed company or you're the only one who's not in the office), these tools may come in useful for you too.

Scheduling

- **World Time Buddy** (www.worktravel.co/worldtimebuddy) helps you schedule a meeting across timezones – you can even send a link to the meeting time in both their country and yours.

- Setting up a meeting with multiple parties often deteriorates into a "I can do Tuesday but not Thursday" / "Oh, I can only do the morning on Wednesday" back-and-forth chat that makes you want to kill yourself.

    Doodle (www.worktravel.co/doodle) helps you find a time that works for everyone without all that faffing around.

    Instead of Doodle, you could install a Gmail extension called Mixmax (www.worktravel.co/mixmax): you can insert time slots straight into a Gmail message. (Mixmax offers a heap of other features including "send later" – mentioned earlier in this chapter.)

- Alternatively, get your clients to book in a time on your calendar. With appointment-booking software **You Can Book Me** (www.worktravel.co/bookme), you can configure the information, dates and times that you're available each week, then send a special link to anyone who wants to book a meeting or phone call with you.

Phone/video calls

Skype

Skype is the default option: most people know it and use it already, a basic account is free, and you can install it on your phone and computer. You can also buy a Skype number in the country where you have clients (www.worktravel.co/skypenumber), which means people can call you from their regular phone at a local rate – useful if you have clients who aren't so good with technology.

Zoom

If you have quite a lot of calls with more than one person at a time (for example, if you have regular catch-ups with a few members of the client company you're working for), it might be worth using Zoom (www.worktravel.co/zoom) instead. The sound quality is superb – even for calls with lots of people, and even when using video. You can also record your meetings and sync with Dropbox, and save a copy of anything that was typed into the text chat box – handy links, passwords, etc.

Zoom is also great for screen sharing: you can screen share documents and video (including audio), as well as co-annotate a document and give someone else remote access to your device during screen sharing.

Zoom's "free" plan is quite generous: up to 25 participants per call, with calls lasting for a maximum of 40 minutes. (If your calls last longer than that, you can always "hang up" and start again. Alternatively, you could upgrade to "Pro", which costs

$9.99 a month for unlimited-length calls and a few extra features.)

There's lots of other software that offers similar features to Zoom. Some people recommend GoToMeeting (www.worktravel.co/gotomeeting) and Join Me (www.worktravel.co/joinme) – which both have free plans and generous trial periods for premium features.

Didlogic

Repetition alert! Didlogic was mentioned briefly in **Chapter 4: Be A Productivity Powerhouse.** *Here I go into a bit more detail and provide some use-cases.*

Didlogic (www.worktravel.co/didlogic) is an altogether more sophisticated (read: complicated but awesome) service. Before getting into the nuts and bolts of how it works, here are the main reasons why you might want to use it:

- You have clients in different countries from where you're living, who'd feel more comfortable calling you on a local number rather than Skype.

- Your wifi is unreliable for phone calls.

Here's how it works:

- You buy a local SIM card for whichever country you're in, and then you buy a Didlogic number through their website (the cost of which varies, but it's in the region of $0.70 a month) that forwards to that local number very inexpensively.

- You can choose a Didlogic number that's based in any country and get it forwarded to any local SIM.

This example of how we use it might help to explain why it's so good:

- Most of our clients are based in the UK, so we have a UK number which anyone can call for the price of a local call. We also have a few clients based in the US, so we have a local US number for them too. Then we just pay a few cents per minute for both numbers to be forwarded to our local SIM card.

- When we're living in Hungary, both numbers will forward to our local Hungarian SIM number. Then when we move to Spain, we'll get a local SIM there and update the forwarding so the same UK and US numbers get forwarded to our Spanish number.

You can do a few other nifty things with Didlogic. For example, Rob sets up his UK cell phone number to forward to his Didlogic number, which in turn forwards to his local cell number. This costs a little extra per minute (because there are two sets of forwarding), but it means that people who tend to call his UK cell don't have to do anything at all: they can reach him on his normal number (without necessarily having to know where he is, if he doesn't want to tell them for whatever reason).

The beauty of this solution is that it doesn't rely on any kind of data connection at all – so even with no wifi and a $5 pay-as-you-go SIM with no data plan, you can receive your calls. For outgoing calls, there's also a "web callback" feature that works out cheaper than Skype in most cases. You *will* need an internet connection for it, but only to kickstart the call; after that it all happens through your phone (so it still comes in handy if you have an unreliable connection that might drop in and out during Skype calls).

Aaand done!

> The Didlogic website is a bit of a mess – and thoroughly useless in helping you get started – so Rob's recorded a quick screencast with an overview of how to set everything up. **Register your purchase of this book at www.worktravel.co to get hold of it!**

Skype To Go

Repetition alert! Skype To Go was mentioned briefly in **Chapter 4: Be A Productivity Powerhouse.** *Here I go into a bit more detail and provide an example of how it can be used.*

Skype To Go (www.worktravel.co/skypetogo) offers a slightly inverted solution to Didlogic. Here's the main reason why you might want to use it:

- You need to call clients in different countries from where you're living (unlike Didlogic, which is more useful for *clients* calling *you*).

- Your wifi is awful or your clients don't use Skype.

It gives you numbers that let you call anyone abroad from any mobile or landline while avoiding international calling charges.

Note that Skype To Go isn't yet available in every single country yet. Here's a list of all the supported countries: www.worktravel.co/skypecountries.

Here's how it works (this example is taken from Skype's website):

Say you live in London and you want to use Skype To Go to call a client who lives in Boston, USA. Add your Boston client as your Skype To Go contact, and Skype will give you a London phone number. When you want to call your client, simply dial that London number from your phone, and your call will be put straight through to your client on their phone in Boston at Skype's low rates.

But what if your client isn't on Skype, or doesn't know how to use it?

That's fine: with a Skype To Go number, you also get an "Access Number" that works like a regular calling card number. When you call your Access Number, you can dial any international number without having to set up the international number as a Skype To Go contact first.

Screen sharing

As mentioned earlier, Zoom has screen sharing options – and

Skype and Google Hangouts offer it too. If you prefer, you can use dedicated screen-sharing software like Screenleap (www.worktravel.co/screenleap) – which is more of a standalone tool that doesn't offer any other features.

Team chat software

If the nature of your project means you're in constant contact and sending things back and forth to your clients, you might prefer to set up a team chat room with them – see the section called "Team chat software" in **Chapter 7: Run The Best Biz** for more information.

Document signing

HelloSign (www.worktravel.co/hellosign) comes in useful if you're asked to sign non-disclosure agreements or contracts from your clients. You can also use it to ask *them* to sign your own documents.

HelloSign is a cloud-based electronic signature tool that allows users to sign, fill out, send, retrieve and save documents paperlessly. Whenever you're sent a document that you're supposed to download, print, sign, scan in and send back, just use HelloSign instead: you can store a digital signature on the site, then use it to sign any document and send it right back. (Alternatively, you can create a digital signature – which is legally binding – using a special tool on the site.)

When it comes to your clients signing *your* documents, they too can upload their own signature or create a digital signature on the site.

HelloSign is free for unlimited self-signatures and up to three signature requests per month, then $15 per month. Check out the tour for a ton of nifty tips and integrations with other apps you use: www.worktravel.co/hellosign.

If you need to fill in complex forms with lots of fields (or you need other people to fill them in for you), take a look at EchoSign (www.worktravel.co/echosign): it costs $15 per month (there's no free plan), but it's a lot more sophisticated.

Mac user alert! You can also sign documents using Preview (although Preview doesn't have the extra features mentioned above).

Conclusion

Freelancing as a digital nomad isn't actually that different from regular freelancing: it just involves a few more logistics and a few nifty little tools and web apps. The key thing is to find the right clients: the ones who don't mind the fact that you're not working in the same country as them.

For more insights into life as a digital nomad freelancer, head to the **Appendix** to read interviews with some of them.

Chapter 6: Hire Like A Champ

We used to simultaneously live by and resent the mantra, "If you want something done right, do it yourself" – and whenever we hired employees or contractors, everything seemed to confirm that we shouldn't have bothered.

It didn't matter what we were hiring for: we just couldn't find the right people or get the best out of them.

We were well aware that *we* were the problem: we were doing something wrong during the hiring process, or once they'd actually started working for us, or both. We didn't know what to do about it though, so we kind of gave up and accepted that we'd spend much of our working lives being annoyed with the people we'd hired. A lot of the time we didn't bother hiring at all: we just tried to do the work ourselves, despite clearly being the worst possible candidates for whatever job we couldn't be bothered to outsource.

Our initial hiring strategy ("don't hire much, and be permanently annoyed with the staff we *do* hire") didn't last for long. We'd been struggling for some time to find fantastic web designers and developers to hire for our copywriting/website business, but then we started up our property management company and myriad other projects – all while trying to invest in our own UK properties from abroad. We had a lot going on – and if we wanted our various businesses and projects to stand a fighting chance, we had to get serious about them. First step: become good at hiring. Even when we couldn't hire in person.

While nothing's perfect yet, we're really getting to grips with "smart hiring" – and our current crop of employees are more wonderful than we could have ever hoped. In the next few sections I run through the hiring processes that are working for us; they should come in handy if you own a business or if you're a freelancer hoping to offload some of your day-to-day commitments.

Hiring remote contractors

There are two main reasons why you might want to hire a contractor:

- If you're looking for someone to do a one-off job for you (Photoshopping out your wrinkles, removing malware, creating a customised Google Apps script, designing a website, etc.), you'll want to hire a contractor.

- If you only need someone for a couple of hours a week, it's easier to just get a contractor rather than go through the effort of looking for and hiring a full-time employee.

(To complicate matters, you could of course have a contractor who's functioning as an employee but just happens to invoice rather than be on the payroll. For this type of arrangement, read the section called "Hiring permanent employees" later in this chapter: the advice there will be more applicable.)

This section covers where to look for contractors, how to hire the best ones, and how to ensure you don't tear your eyebrows out through the stress of managing them.

That last bit really happened to Rob:

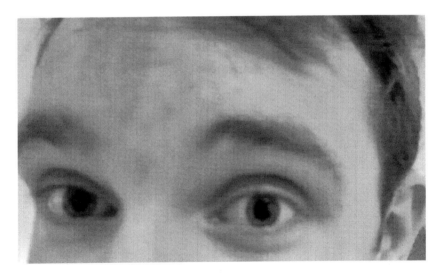

Resources for hiring contractors

There are many, many online marketplaces and websites for hiring contractors – and we've used a lot of them.

The one we've had the most success with is Upwork (formerly

Elance/oDesk):

- **Upwork** (www.worktravel.co/upwork) is a marketplace where you can hire freelancers in a number of different fields. We've hired programmers, web designers, book designers, editors, malware experts, long-term virtual assistants, data-entry assistants and a whole lot more from Upwork. Sometimes the jobs are small and standalone; sometimes we actually hire the contractor on an hourly "wage" for long-term work.

There are others – like Guru (www.worktravel.co/guru) and Freelancer (www.worktravel.co/freelancer) – and they're worth checking out if you can't find the people you're looking for on Upwork.

For developer-specific tasks, check out:

- **Gigster** (www.worktravel.co/gigster). I haven't used it, but it offers a super-duper quick way (including a "guaranteed quote in 5 minutes") to get a developer started on your project.

If you're after quick, one-off design jobs and you're happy to pay a slight premium (although *nothing* compared to what you'd pay an agency), check out these sites:

- **99 Designs** (www.worktravel.co/99designs) is a graphic design marketplace. As the customer, you can solicit designers to submit designs for products like websites, logos, book covers and brochures. You can then choose the best design from the pool of submitted entries, and the selected designer will win a cash payment. (You can choose from different pricing packages depending on the quality of work you're after. You pay upfront, but if no one submits a design that you like, you get a refund.)

It really is an excellent service. While you'll generally get cheaper designers on Upwork, 99 Designs is a much quicker process: you commission once and get tens of options to choose from. It's also still much cheaper than commissioning a high-quality design agency.

(Note that Freelancer also offers a similar service, called "Contests".)

- **Crowdspring** (www.worktravel.co/crowdspring) works a lot like 99 Designs, but it also has a "naming" option: you can get people to help you name your product or business.

For small, personal-assistant-esque tasks, you could also consider:

- **Fancy Hands** (www.worktravel.co/fancyhands) is useful if you're looking for US-based virtual assistants. You pay a monthly or yearly fee and in return they'll do a certain number of small, discrete tasks for you. Their capabilities extend far beyond typical data-entry tasks. Here are some examples from their website:

    - "Set up a meeting with my accountant (cc'ed

here). If she's paying, let's go to Balthazar, otherwise, let's do it at our office."

- "Call TD Bank and ask how many checks I can use for free on a standard personal account (I don't want any more fees!) If you need to patch me in for my account details, please call me on my cell."

- "I'd like to get rental car quotes from 3 different companies at LAX. I'd be picking up next Saturday morning and keeping the car for 4 days. I'd like a convertible but also might take an SUV. Please find out the prices and brands for both options."

- "Can you proofread this article that I wrote and send me any edits? Make your edits in red so I know what you've done."

Tips for hiring contractors

These tips apply specifically to the marketplace-style websites mentioned in the previous section – Upwork, Freelancer and the like.

Write a clear job description

Here are some real-life not-so-clear job descriptions that have been posted on Upwork:

- "Design a website for home and garden ecommerce.

Must be skilled in marketing and seo. Must live in southern California."

- "The objective is perform css work for HomePage for web site. The requirements are knowledge in CSS,XHTML, and HTML5."

- "I need a website to sell products and will need paypal? but it won't be so complicated? home page, products page, Contact page, and About us page?or something with some company details?"

Descriptions like that might be quick to write, but they attract vague, unqualified responses and proposals. The best people won't bother to reply at all, because they know that someone will be a pain to work for if they can't even communicate what they want properly.

Other applicants will bid with an inflated price because they'll anticipate lots of back-and-forth trying to figure out what the heck it is they're meant to be working on.

Depending on the nature of the task, there are a few things you can do to make your job description as clear as possible:

- If it's an admin-type task, do a bit of it yourself first – it'll help you write precise instructions, find exceptions, and get a sense for how long it should take someone to complete.

- If it's a design task, include examples of work you like

and what you like about it.

- If it's a programming task that involves fixing something that's broken or implementing a feature that's on another site, consider recording a screencast where you show what's wrong or what you want.

Writing a comprehensive job description will save you time at every other step of the process, so it's worth getting it right.

Here are some job descriptions that we've posted on Upwork recently:

Job description 1: "Copy documents across from one Google account to another"

I need approximately 50 documents to be migrated from one Google Drive account to another, and the links within them fixed. For various reasons this can't be done automatically so needs to be done by hand.

Step 1:

I will give you access to the original directory, using your own Google account.

You will then log into the target account in a separate browser and re-create every document individually by creating a new document, then copying across the document title and document contents.

The end result will be that the files in the new account will be identical to the files in the old account.

Step 2:

Many of the documents contain links to each other, which will be broken by re-creating the documents.

You will therefore need to go through each new document in turn, see what internal links it contains, and update these links so they point to the new version of the target file.

Each document contains an average of 3 links. There is one document that links to every other document, so has about 50 links.

Job description 2: "Synchronize a PowerPoint presentation to an audio file"

I have a 1-hour audio file (WAV) which needs to be synchronised with a PowerPoint presentation (PPT). There is a separate document which specifies the exact timings in the audio when the presentation needs to be advanced to the next slide.

This could either be achieved by recording the screen while you listen to the audio and manually advancing the slides at the correct time (in which case it will take exactly one hour!), or you could use another method if you prefer.

The final output should:

- Be an MP4 file

- 1280 x 720 dimensions

- Show the presentation full-screen, so you can't see anything but the slides

- Have clear audio that is not distorted, with no background noise introduced (so make sure audio isn't being captured from your microphone)

Invite people with star quality

All the freelancing sites will allow you to actively browse and invite contractors to your job rather than just sit around and hope they find you. This can be a huge time-saver: if one of your invitees responds with a price you like, you can just hire them and save reading through any other applications.

Inviting contractors makes particular sense for design jobs, because you can look through portfolios and get a sense for whose style you like. But it also works for any other kind of job. If you can find a few people with a strong portfolio, great reviews and an hourly rate that's acceptable to you, invite them all and you might be able to shortcut the hiring process.

Filter ruthlessly

Whatever job you post, you'll almost certainly end up with tens of applications of a *very* variable standard. Some contractors even use special software to automatically bid on every job that comes up in a certain category.

To avoid spending hours going through them all, you'll have to be brutal with your filtering so that you can narrow the field to find a few candidates to speak with in more detail. Your own criteria will vary, but I tend to eliminate the following:

- Anyone with a "job success" rating of 90% or lower (or a star rating of 4.7 or lower)

- Anyone who responds with paragraphs of boilerplate about their skills, but doesn't mention anything specific about the job

- Anyone who quotes what seems like an insanely low price for the work involved (because they probably haven't read it properly)

- Anyone who addresses me as "Dear Sir"

I might miss the odd gem, but speed is the name of the game.

This may seem unnecessarily harsh – especially considering my freelancing career started on Upwork (formerly Elance/oDesk), and at one point I had absolutely no work history. I *will* break some of these rules of thumb if someone contacts me with a particularly engaging application and seems to have a firm grasp of what's required of them.

One more tip: somewhere in your job description, ask the candidates to tell you something random about themselves. In the past I've asked them to tell me their favourite type of cheese, their favourite animal at the zoo, and their shoe size. It's a simple way to filter out those candidates who either haven't read the job properly or are using automated software to bid for jobs. I also like it because it's nice to work with people who have a sense of humour, and some of the responses I receive are hilarious!

Hourly or fixed price?

You usually have the option to specify whether you want to pay your contractor an hourly rate or a fixed price.

While it's *kind of* "totally up to you" and no one's going to put you in prison for choosing one over the other, it's not *really* totally up to you – not if you want to hire in a way that best suits your needs.

Here are some things to consider:

Choose hourly if...

- The scope of the project is uncertain at the start – for example, if you want a website created from scratch but you haven't yet nailed down every aspect of your requirements (perhaps because you want your contractor's input). Going with an hourly rate means you can both readjust expectations and requirements as you go along.

- You want to hire someone for an ongoing project or work. For example, if you want someone to do customer service for your company for eight hours a week, it makes more sense to pay by the hour.

- You want to get started RIGHT NOW! Jobs can get

started pretty much instantly, because there's no need to map out every detail of the project too greatly in advance.

Choose fixed price if...

- You have a well-defined, standalone job that you want someone to do. For example, getting a book cover designed, Photoshopping 30 photos, or creating a certain number of redirects from your old site to your new one. (If the scope changes, things aren't completely set in stone: you *can* adjust the budget. But it definitely helps if you have a fairly firm idea of what you want done at the start.)

- You have a fixed budget and you're not prepared to risk going over it.

Fixed price is also useful for comparing the proposals of the prospective contractors: you can take a look at their work, their levels of experience and their reviews and decide if someone is worth paying more for – and it's not your problem how long it actually takes them. With hourly, one person could be $15 an hour and someone else could bid $20 an hour, but it's harder to figure out who'll actually end up costing you more.

If you're searching around desperately for a middle ground, there is one… kind of. You can set up a fixed-price job but but add in a bunch of milestones. This gets covered more in the next section.

And remember...

You don't *actually* have to do all the hiring and managing yourself if you don't want to! If you take on a lot of contractors, you can delegate the job of hiring to someone else – an employee or even a contractor whose sole job it is to hire for you! Just make sure that the person knows *exactly* what you're looking for and has access to your procedures and strategies for finding the best people.

Quick tips for managing remote contractors

Set "milestones"

On most marketplace sites, you're allowed to set "milestones" – key dates in the job schedule in which work can be reviewed, approved and paid for. Every job has at least one milestone: the final result. But you can set up interim milestones along the way too.

When you work with a new contractor, you might want to set a milestone after a very short period of work (one hour of data entry or ten images out of 100, for example). If there's been any misunderstanding, you can set them straight and there won't be much work to undo.

You can also set milestones throughout the course of your job. You don't *have* to link them to payments, but if you do you'll know that the contractor won't be able to request the next set amount of money until they've completed what they were meant to have done.

Here's some useful information about milestones: www.worktravel.co/milestones.

Be responsive, communicative and helpful

A few years ago, a Sri Lankan contractor I'd hired on Upwork suggested we "have a Skype call and do a screen share" so that I could better explain the problem I wanted him to fix.

My first thought was: "Oh the terror! Talking to a complete stranger who I've only just hired... how do I start the conversation? What happens if I can't answer his questions? Will I be able to understand him – and will he understand me?"

My second thought was: "Hang on... I thought I'd hired an *expert* who could fix my problems without any more help from me. What's going on here?"

And then Rob told me to stop being such an arse and just arrange a damn Skype call with the nice man. Turns out my contractor had some valid questions – questions which actually showed just how much of an expert he was. Our Skype call allowed me to show him (quickly and easily) exactly what problem I needed help with, and it also helped us build a bit of a rapport.

It doesn't *have* to be Skype – you can communicate with your contractor over email/internal messaging if you prefer, or you can even record a screencast using software like Screencast-o-matic: www.worktravel.co/screencast. But don't just expect that they'll be able to get on with the job with zero input from you.

Pay up and review well

Given that finding good contractors is the most time-consuming part of the process, once you've found a winner you'll want to stick with them for future jobs.

Just as in a "proper" business, the best way to hold onto good staff is to treat them well. On a marketplace site like Upwork, that means paying quickly and being generous with ratings (and being friendly in communicating, of course).

Being generous with bonuses helps too. Paying a bonus equal to one hour at their normal rate (or a small proportion of their project fee) will make little difference to your finances, but could propel you to the top of the pile when you've got a job you need doing quickly next time.

Hiring permanent employees

When hiring a "remote" or "distributed" team of employees, you won't be able to conduct in-person interviews – which is what would normally give you a sense of what a person is like and whether they'll be a good fit.

That doesn't mean hiring is hard; it's just a case of doing things a bit differently and being more thorough in your approach. In this section I explain in detail the hiring processes that have worked well for us and other distributed teams. First though, a quick look at the the *many* benefits of working in this way…

Is hiring a "remote team" just a necessary evil of this lifestyle?

As a digital nomad business owner, you'll have little choice but to hire people who live in a different location from you. You *could* have an office in one part of the world and insist that all your staff work from there even if you don't (and you could hire a manager to oversee everything), but let's assume you're not going to do that.

So... you're going to be hiring candidates who aren't necessarily from your home country, who'll need to work from home (or make use of a coworking space/cafe if they want to) and who'll have to use their own computers. What's more, they'll often be in a different timezone from both you and their co-workers, and you'll never (or rarely) see them in person.

If you're struggling to appreciate the immediate benefits of this arrangement, here are a few to get you started:

- "Local" or "location dependent" businesses need an office, which means rent, taxes, copiers, printers, computers, heating, electricity, flip charts, coffee machines, stationery, muesli, cookies... With a remote team, you don't have to pay for any of it.

  You're also saving on hassle. When the ping-pong paddle goes AWOL or the A/C shuts down, *someone* has to deal with it. These problems disappear when you don't have an office.

- You can hire brilliant people – not just people who live nearby or would be willing to do the commute. This benefit should not be underestimated. When hiring for positions in our property management company, our only requirement was that employees lived in the UK (because they need knowledge of the UK property industry and will have to speak to our UK-based clients during regular office hours). But they can live *anywhere* in the country – which means we've been able to pick the very best. Future roles at the company could easily be filled by people living elsewhere in the world.

- If your business will have customers around the world, then hiring employees around the world is beneficial: hire enough people in different timezones and you have 24/7 customer support without needing to negotiate night shifts or extra pay.

    Another "timezone benefit" is that your staff will often be working, fixing problems and troubleshooting while you sleep. Then as soon as you're up you can see what they've done and give them feedback or answers.

- There's none of the office politics that tends to plague most working environments. And it helps that no one's sleeping with anyone else either: you don't have to deal with the hassle and tremendous loss of productivity when the relationship goes awry and they can't bear to be near each other.

- You HAVE to focus heavily on hiring self-motivated and

productive people – something all employers need to do more of, but don't because it's easier to look at a list of achievements on a résumé instead. Hiring people with the right attitude will pay dividends later on. I explain how to do this later on in this chapter.

- It IS possible to have a happy, friendly working environment – even when you're all thousands of miles away from each other. I explain how later on in this chapter.

Convinced? I certainly hope so. Next up: how to hire superb staff.

Resources for hiring remote employees

It's a good thing you're not reading this book (and I'm not writing it) a few years ago: back then, there were few resources for hiring remote employees. Thankfully, that's all changed.

Here are some tools and resources for finding your new family of staff members:

- **"Mom" job boards** are our saviour. We've hired an entire team of permanent employees from a job board in the UK called Working Mums (www.worktravel.co/workingmums). The women (and a few men) looking for jobs on the site often prefer to work from home so that they can be there for their children. From what we've seen, they have a wealth of experience in their particular industry but had to step off the corporate ladder when having kids – and now they're extremely keen to have a part-time or full-time remote job doing something they love. A similar website in the US is Hire My Mom (www.worktravel.co/hiremymom).

- **Specialised "remote work" job boards** are currently most useful if you're looking for techie or customer-support-related employees or contractors (although there are a few other jobs on there too). When more companies start to become remote, this will change. In the meantime, it's well worth posting a job if you have an opening for something like a programmer or designer – or if you're looking to fill a helpdesk role.

    There are many remote job boards out there where you can post, such as:

    - Remotive (www.worktravel.co/remotive): full-time remote jobs.

    - Remote OK (www.worktravel.co/remoteok): full-time, one-off, part-time, etc. jobs.

    - WFH.io (www.worktravel.co/wfh) remote jobs solely in the technology space.

    - We Work Remotely (www.worktravel.co/wework): has a few more non-technie jobs compared to the others. Most of the jobs are full-time, permanent roles.

- Authentic Jobs (www.worktravel.co/authentic): doesn't just list remote jobs, but there's a handy filter for people looking for them. Has a wide range of freelance, contract, full-time and part-time jobs available.

- **Specialist virtual assistant (VA)/"outsourcing" sites** work in one of two ways: either you submit your requirements and a team finds you your perfect virtual assistant, or you scour their directory looking for suitable candidates to interview. Either way, there's usually a bit of a chunky upfront cost.

  Most of the virtual assistants are from Asia, which means they're a lot cheaper than hiring someone from the US, Europe or Australia. You can hire for anything from data entry to design and development – and you can even find some with good enough English to provide decent customer service. The quality of work *can* be superb, but we've heard stories about some staff members not meeting expectations.

- **Upwork** (www.worktravel.co/upwork) can be used for ongoing work too. The benefit of using this site is that you can hire someone for a one-off job, see how they perform, then invite them to a more permanent, ongoing role.

Tips for hiring remote employees

Until a year or so ago, we didn't have much experience with

hiring long-term employees. Apart from a staff writer and a virtual assistant (both of whom have been with us for some time), everyone else we hired had been short-term or one-off. As a copywriting company, we simply didn't need anyone else.

But when we started up Yellow Lettings, we needed some permanent employees.

Today we have seven members of staff and counting. We've never met a single one of them in person, but we feel like we know and understand them – and they us. They do incredible work for us every day, and we'd be stuck without them.

Surprisingly, we've only had a couple of hiring mishaps since starting up this business – and they were right at the start. The problem with our initial hires was that we trusted our "gut instinct" way too much. As soon as we realised where we were going wrong, we told our guts to stick to the day job and created some finely tuned processes to do the work of finding ideal candidates instead.

I'm not saying that gut instincts are unimportant: they definitely have their uses. These uses come later though – not right at the start of the hiring process, when you don't know which candidates are actually capable of doing the job. You need to narrow down your candidates to those who definitely fulfil your criteria, and *then* get rid of anyone who you "just feel would probably be a nincompoop".

The remainder of this chapter explains the hiring process and principles that work for us:

- Know what you're hiring for.

- Write a great job post.

- Have a thorough "stage 1" application process to help you narrow down your candidates.

- Interview your shortlisted candidates – with questions that focus heavily on discovering their attitudes to work.

1: Know what you're hiring for

It's amazing how much we *didn't* focus on this in the past. Hiring a "systems coordinator" or "lettings manager" isn't enough: you need to be clear in your own mind what you want that person to achieve in their role, and what their daily/weekly responsibilities will be. As a result, you'll be able to write a far more accurate job post – which will attract a better selection of prospects.

It also means you can create some "key performance indicators" (KPIs) to evaluate your new employee's progress in their role – far more useful and objective than "a feeling" that they're not working as well as they should be. For example, if you're hiring someone to manage your customer services team, one of your KPIs might be customer satisfaction – which means you know you need to measure this too (through surveys, phone calls, etc.).

For more examples of KPIs, visit www.worktravel.co/kpi.

2: Write a great job post

Here are some things you should include in your job post:

- **An accurate and detailed explanation of the position.** It's no use saying you want an "experienced marketer" or a "great copywriter" – those descriptions are far too broad and will mean different things to different people. You need to explain what sort of work they'll be expected to do on a daily basis, what sort of results you want to see from them once they're in the role, and what sort of experience you expect them to have (if any).

- **A brief description of your business.** In order for the applicant to get a full understanding of the position they're applying for, it's helpful for them to know a bit of background information about your business.

- **Hours and pay.** And importantly: flexibility of hours. You might not need them to work a regular 9-to-5, so specify how many hours they're expected to work, and how much flexibility they have when it comes to choosing which hours. (You might prefer not to include pay in your job post, and that's fine. We like to have everything out in the open so that we're not wasting our or their time with incorrect assumptions about pay. But plenty of companies have their reasons for not divulging this information.)

- **Weekly/monthly/regular requirements.** Will they be

expected to have any regular catch-up calls or meetings with you? Will they need to have quarterly reviews, or provide a detailed report of the work they've done each week?

- **Location.** Do they need to live anywhere specific – or will it be helpful for them if they do? (For example, they might have to be in regular contact with US-based clients, so it makes sense for them to live there – or at least in the same timezone – too.)

- **Instructions on how to apply.** If you just get them to send you a résumé, it'll be difficult to whittle them down to a shortlist. There are many other more efficient and effective ways of getting candidates to apply – and I go through some of them in the next section. We always get our candidates to answer a couple of questions – questions that (while relatively simple) give us a great insight into whether they'll be a good match for our company.

3: Don't just ask for a résumé and cover letter

As I was saying…

We never ask candidates to just send in a résumé and cover letter: we'd find it almost impossible to decide which ones should "go through" to the interview stage of the process, and that means we'd end up interviewing a load of unsuitable people when we could have been working on other things. Or sunbathing.

Also, a résumé indicating a lack of experience might mean that the person isn't put through when actually they'd be worth a punt – if only we'd asked them a few more questions to make us realise that.

The nature of the application process will vary depending on the job you're hiring for, but below are some real-life case studies for inspiration.

One last thing before you read the case studies: regardless of the role you're hiring for, it's worth paying attention to how well your prospects can *write*.

Even if they're applying for roles that require very little writing, there's a good chance they'll be writing to *you* and other members of the team frequently – over email, internal messaging, etc. They can't just bounce up to your desk when they have a question or concern – they'll need to write to you, if only to ask for a Skype call to talk it through.

People who "can't write" in this context aren't people with poor grammar or punctuation; they're people who struggle to put their point across quickly and effectively. They might accidentally appear rude to other team members because their messages are short and emotionless. Or they might confuse everyone with convoluted and impenetrable sentences.

Employing someone who can't write – even if they're *excellent* for the role itself – can be a time-consuming and morale-undermining mistake.

Back to those case studies:

Case study 1: super PA

At the bottom of our job posting (for a PA role we needed to fill), we asked people to apply by visiting a page on our website – from where they could fill in a short form. In the form we asked their name and email address, as well as two trickier questions. There was also a button for them to upload their résumé.

The trickier questions were:

1. *"If we interviewed people you've worked with in the past, what would you expect them to say are your strengths and weaknesses?"*

    We asked this because we wanted someone who could be honest about themselves and areas in which they needed to improve. We also wanted to make sure that their weaknesses wouldn't be completely detrimental to our business! A PA with bad organisational skills would be a disaster, for example.

2. *"Describe a complex challenge you've had to coordinate."*

    We wanted evidence of their "can do" abilities. (A few candidates wrote things like, "I organised my son's fourth birthday party, which was really quite difficult because some of the children were vegetarian and I needed to make sure that they had nice meals too." They didn't get through to the next round.)

But most importantly, we wanted to see evidence that they could write well. Our PA would be expected to email people constantly, and we needed to make sure they had a friendly style and could explain things clearly and concisely. Many of them were able to explain a genuinely complex challenge in a really easy-to-understand (and often funny) way, and those people went through to the next round.

> If you'd like to see the entire job post (as well as the application form) for our "Super PA", register your purchase of this book at www.worktravel.co.

Case study 2: staff writer

When we needed to hire staff writers for our property investment magazine, we directed them to a page on our site which asked them to complete a writing task as part of their application:

"For us, style is more important than experience – so as well as a brief CV [résumé], we'd like to see how you perform on the type of task you'd be doing in the role.

So for your application, please listen to [this episode of The Property Podcast] and write a 400-word article for our blog based on it.

You can summarise the entire episode, pick out one point to explore in more detail, or whatever you want – it's up to you! We're mainly looking at your creativity, technique, and ability to replicate the tone of the podcast in writing.

Submit your article to [email address], and don't forget to include a CV or covering letter so we can learn something about you too."

Case study 3: business development role

When Zapier (a webapp automation service) was hiring for its business development position, candidates had to complete a short series of written exercises to test their abilities. They were also asked to write a sample pitch email to a partner rather than supply a cover letter.

Here are some of the exercises they asked candidates to complete:

- *"How would you prioritize these upcoming integrations and why? Office 365, Flickr, Marketo, Wunderlist, Pocket, Ontraport, Hootsuite, and Joomla"*

- *"How would you get in touch with the following people (don't actually contact them). Editor at Lifehacker, Andrew Warner, CEO of Slack"*

- *"If you could launch one new integration on Zapier, what app would you choose? What would you do to make the launch successful?"*

Case study 4: quality assurance engineer

Wildbit is a company that creates web products for businesses. Here are some of the questions it asked candidates who wanted to apply for the job:

- "Which design patterns do you prefer when writing automated tests?"

- "Do you enjoy and see the value in manual testing just as much as you do with automated?" (Yes/No)

- "What are some of your favorite testing tools at the moment?"

- "Have you worked remotely? If so, describe your work space."

- "Tell us more! Favorite tech books, your own writing, code samples, GitHub profile, etc."

4: Interview your best candidates

By this stage you should have pared down your candidates. If you still have quite a few to choose between, you *could* provide them with an extra task before interviewing them. Interviewing is pretty time-consuming and draining (especially when you consider the prep work you'll have to do before each one), so having an extra filter could come in handy.

Regardless, at some stage you'll need to conduct interviews. It's hard to give advice on the types of interview questions you'll want to ask, because all businesses are so different. But there's one general overriding principle that applies to most hiring situations:

Your questions should help you discover each person's

attitude and personality, and that's what you want to hire for.

Don't take this too literally: if you've got a really eager guy on your hands who can't code for toffee, it's probably not the best idea to hire him for your new "Grindr for Bungee Jumpers" app. But if the guy has a fair bit of background experience, isn't necessarily the best in his field, but is mega keen to work with you and help you grow, don't discount him just because he doesn't have the most impressive skills out of everyone you've interviewed.

The attitude you're looking for will depend on your business and what you want to get out of your employee. First you need to figure out which attitudinal attributes you're looking for; then you need to ask the right interview questions to figure out if prospects have these attributes.

(In our experience, it's quite tricky trying to figure out if candidates have the "right attitude" before the interview, especially if they aren't – and don't need to be – great writers.)

Case study: lettings manager

Before we hired our lettings manager for Yellow Lettings, we discovered a website (and book) called Topgrading (www.worktravel.co/topgrading). It allows you to select certain attributes that you want in your employees, and then it helps you formulate interview questions. The questions are all phrased to elicit answers that will reveal if your prospective employee has the attitude you're looking for.

While you of course don't need to use Topgrading (or any other hiring resource), it'll still be useful to go online and look for information and tips on "hiring for attitude".

We decided that we wanted to hire for the following attributes:

- Judgement/decision-making
- Experience in the industry
- Resourcefulness
- Organisation
- Independence
- Customer focus

You'll see that lots of these focus on "attitude" rather than "skills".

Below are some of the questions we asked interviewees during their interview. They're really quite tough, and some of them cleverly prevent the applicant from assuming what the "right" answer should be. Take a look at questions 1) and 11), for example.

Bear in mind that we were looking to hire a critically important member of staff for our business, so we needed to be exceptionally thorough with our interview questions. You may not have to ask *quite* so many tough questions if you don't feel they're necessary for the role!

Judgement/decision-making:

1: Please describe your decision-making approach. Are you decisive and quick, but sometimes too quick, or are you more thorough, but sometimes too slow? Are you intuitive or do you go purely with the facts?

2: What maxims do you live by?

3: What are a couple of the most challenging decisions you have made recently?

Experience in the industry:

4: How would you rate yourself at…

- Handling tenants?
- Handling landlords?
- Admin?
- New technology?

5: Looking back at your career, what were your most and least successful jobs?

Resourcefulness:

6: What actions would you take in the first weeks, should you join Yellow Lettings?

7: Give an example of a circumstance in which you were

expected to do a certain thing and you ended up going beyond the call of duty?

Organisation:

8: Describe a complex challenge you had to coordinate.

9: When was the last time you missed a significant deadline?

10: Everyone procrastinates at times. What are the kind of things that you procrastinate on?

Independence:

11: Do you believe in asking for forgiveness rather than permission, or are you inclined to be sure your bosses are in full agreement before acting?

12: How much supervision do you need or want?

Customer focus:

13: If we interviewed past clients of yours, what would you expect them to say are your strengths and weaknesses?

14: What is your track record in both acquiring and retaining clients?

We graded everyone on each answer in a spreadsheet, and also took down brief notes to remind ourselves about them. While it definitely wasn't a case of "the one with the highest grade wins", those grades and notes definitely helped us remember what we liked, admired and were impressed by when thinking back through all our interviewees.

We also gave candidates the opportunity to ask *us* about the role; some of their questions were extremely insightful and impressive – which helped make our decision-making even easier.

5: Listen to your gut

Once you've interviewed some people for the role and you've cast aside the ones who clearly aren't right, you should have a shortlist of candidates who are all perfect.

And NOW's the time to listen to that gut of yours!

Who can you imagine yourself working with?

Who *might* drive you insane?

Who do you just feel "isn't right"?

You have nothing left to go on but your gut instinct!

6: Consider having a short initial contract period

The founders of software application Buffer run a remote team, and they've initiated a 45-day contract period with all new recruits. It provides them with a way of figuring out if people are self-motivated and a right fit for the team before committing. Here's more information on what they call "Buffer Bootcamp": www.worktravel.co/bootcamp.

We don't do this ourselves, but it could be something to consider – especially if you've never hired before.

Note: there's an interview with Buffer employee Carolyn Kopprasch in the Appendix – where she talks more about Buffer's hiring processes.

Before you hire... research local employment laws

When you hire internationally, the employment laws in each employee's country may differ from the one where your business is set up.

If you want to put them on the payroll, you'll need to do some digging into whether you're responsible for paying local payroll taxes and employer insurance premiums in their country of residence, for example.

Alternatively, you could hire them on full-time contracts – which is something Buffer does with all its non-US-based staff (www.worktravel.co/hiringatbuffer). But even then, do some research first and ensure you take legal advice for each country in which you hire.

Conclusion

Hiring can feel like the world's biggest ball-ache at times, and remote hiring isn't exempted from that. I do, however, think that it has strong benefits over traditional methods.

Hiring people without meeting them in person will force you to be more thorough, and to focus on things like writing ability and phone manner (which are often important attributes of *any* employee). And as a result, you're more likely to make good hiring decisions the first time – which will at least save you from future firing-related hassles.

Chapter 7: Run The Best Biz

Hiring is just the start: your work is definitely not over as soon as they've digitally signed the contract and emailed you a virtual high-five. But – just as with hiring – running your business is very different when you're doing it remotely.

In this chapter I explain what you need to think about and how to ensure you have a great company culture that's well organised and big on communication.

First though, a quick general note about the chapter: I've tried to focus solely on what you as a remote business owner need to know about and consider. I haven't included any information that *all* business owners will need to think about – like maternity leave, sick days, promotions and resignations.

Communication

Working with a distributed team means you can't just "grab" someone "for five minutes", or lean over to ask them a question. You can't thrash out ideas by taking it in turns with the flip chart and marker pen. You can't bond over your joint love of *The Bachelorette* by the water cooler (do people still do that, or is it just a cliché these days?) And you can't see the looks of delight or misery or frustration on their faces.

That doesn't mean it's *harder* to communicate with your employees – just that you have to go about it in a different way.

Here are some communication tools and tips to help you get started. (You might also want to head to the **Appendix** for interviews with other digital nomads who manage or work in distributed teams.)

Team chat software

It's likely that much of your communication with staff will be in written form. While you'll need to actually speak to each other too (which I discuss in a little bit), sending synchronous messages is often the easiest way to correspond – especially if you're on different sides of the world.

If you're going to be talking to your staff frequently throughout the day, consider using a team chat app rather than email. With email, messages are likely to get lost amid all your *other* emails, and it's much harder to ask for or receive quick answers. With team chat, everything is a running conversation between everyone – which means that if you're not around but someone else can answer a question, they'll be able to do so. Team chat also means that everyone knows what's going on – and there's no risk of forgetting to cc them into an email that they might want to know about.

We don't just use team chat for work-related stuff: there's also a lot of general chatter about the weekend, TV shows, pets, travel and so on interspersed in there too. Whether your own team chat is a "work-only zone" or not is up to you: what you talk about will set the tone for everyone else.

Here are some other benefits to team chat apps:

- You can alert people when you're talking directly to them, usually by using the "@" sign. It means they'll get a pop-up notification, or an email alert if they're offline.

- You can usually set up different "rooms" or areas for different parts of your business. If the software development team never has to know what the sales team is up to, for example, you can just create separate areas for them within the software.

- You can share files through the software too – rather than email them separately.

- Team chat apps often include conference call technology and video chat, screen sharing, integration with cloud storage services, and more.

- Search functionality tends to be pretty good, enabling you to easily refer back to conversations you had in the past.

- If you ever hire a one-off contractor, you can add them to your team chat while they're with you, enabling them to easily communicate with the rest of your team. (You can also set up a special room for them and the people they're working with, if you don't want them having access to everything that goes on.)

There are lots of team chat software options available, but the two most popular are HipChat and Slack. They both fulfil the same need, but have various differences when it comes to nifty little add-ons and integrations with other software. To find out which one is best for you…

1. Take the Slack tour (www.worktravel.co/slack), and see which other services it integrates with (www.worktravel.co/slack2).

2. Take the HipChat tour (www.worktravel.co/hipchat), and see which other services it integrates with (www.worktravel.co/hipchat2).

3. Google "Slack vs HipChat" and see what people are saying.

4. Compare the pricing (both offer generous "free" options, which you can start with before moving up to paid accounts).

    - Slack pricing: www.worktravel.co/slack3

    - HipChat pricing: www.worktravel.co/hipchat3

Structured meetings and ad-hoc calls

Repetition alert! Many (but not all) of the tools in this section are also mentioned in **Chapter 5: Freelance From Anywhere.**

Sometimes it's easier for you and your team to just have a quick call about something rather than try to explain it in writing.

You also might want to have regular meeting/check-in phone calls with your employees, to keep them accountable and give them a time when they can bring up issues that might not get mentioned over team chat.

At our company we decided to have weekly all-staff meetings. And because we don't spend as much time speaking to them as we would if we were in the same office, we try hard to get the most out of these weekly calls by following a structure that Rob stole from Mastering the Rockefeller Habits by Verne Harnish (www.worktravel.co/rockefeller):

- **Personal updates.** As silly as you like.

- **Client feedback.** What have our clients said about us that's positive? What has someone been unhappy about, which we can learn from?

- **Reviewing KPIs and quarterly goals.** We look at our most important numbers, and track how we're progressing towards our targets.

- **Individual issues.** We work through a list of talking points that we've all thrown on our joint to-do list throughout the week.

We then make sure that every item discussed ends with an action item assigned to a particular person. As Rob likes to remind us all over and over again: "Nothing ever happens in an organisation until it appears on someone's weekly to-do list." (He stole that from Mastering the Rockefeller Habits too.) Even if it's just "Think about a list of options to solve this issue and report back next week," someone needs to take responsibility – otherwise we could spend time complaining about something without getting any closer to resolving it.

There are lots of tools out there to help you arrange and have these phone calls; here are some of them:

Tools for scheduling meetings

- World Time Buddy (www.worktravel.co/worldtimebuddy) lets you see what the local time is across the various timezones of your meeting attendees. You can then click on a time when everyone will be awake and working, and send a link to all recipients to show them what time the meeting will be in their respective countries. It's completely free to use.

- Regular calls can be added to your employees' Google Calendar (www.worktravel.co/calendar), with pop-up and/or email reminders if necessary.

    Tip: pick ONE timezone and use it to schedule all your Google Calendar meetings. It means that when you move in and out of timezones (either by moving country or because of daylight savings), Google Calendar will automatically update your own calendar events accordingly. A catchup call could show up as being at 10am when you're in New York, 11am the following week when the city moves into daylight savings, then 4pm when you travel to London.

We schedule all our meetings in UTC (Coordinated Universal Time) because it seems easiest and the most logical: UTC is a universal "reference" time: your own timezone will be with reference to UTC. For example, New York during daylight savings is "UTC -4" (UTC minus four hours) and "UTC -5" during the rest of the year. UTC time is the same worldwide and doesn't vary regarding the timezone or daylight saving time.

Tools for having phone calls

Skype and Google Hangouts are the default go-to options for international phone calls, but the sound quality isn't great (especially for calls involving more than two people) and there are often huge delays. Recording the call (which you might want to do) isn't a cinch either.

Here are a couple of alternatives:

Zoom

Zoom (www.worktravel.co/zoom) is a web and video conferencing service. The sound quality is superb – even for calls with lots of people. If you want to keep video on, the video quality is great too. You can also record your meetings and sync with Dropbox – useful for giving other people in the business instant access to any information that was disseminated during the call, and handy for people who were meant to attend but unable to be there for whatever reason. You can also save a copy of anything that was typed into the text chat box – handy links, passwords, etc.

Zoom is also great for screen sharing: one person can give a presentation or provide a lesson on something by sharing their screen with other people in the call.

The "free" plan is quite generous: up to 25 participants per call, with calls lasting for a maximum of 40 minutes. (If your calls tend to last longer than that, you can always "hang up" and start again. Alternatively, you could upgrade to "Pro", which costs $9.99 a month for unlimited-length calls and a few extra features.)

Zoom isn't the only contender in this category – there are plenty of others that you might want to check out too. Other people recommend GoToMeeting (www.worktravel.co/gotomeeting) and Join Me (www.worktravel.co/joinme) – which both have free plans and generous trial periods for premium features.

Appear.in

Appear.in (www.worktravel.co/appear) is a much lighter-weight (and free) alternative to Zoom. You simply visit the website, select a "room name" (like appear.in/eager-mosquito or appear.in/arrogant-weasel – they'll helpfully suggest fun names for you), then send the link to everyone who needs to attend.

You all end up in a video conference "room" together, although it's possible to switch off the video if you prefer.

And that's about it! The limitations with Appear.in are related to its functionality: there's not much else you can do with it besides that which I've already mentioned. (Although you *can* do screen sharing if you install an extension.) But the quality is fantastic – far, far better than Skype or Google Hangouts – and it's extremely easy to use.

Screen sharing

To share your screen with members of your team, you can use Skype, Google Hangouts, Zoom or Appear.in – all mentioned in the previous section. Alternatively, you could use dedicated screen-sharing software like Screenleap (www.worktravel.co/screenleap) – which is more of a standalone tool that doesn't offer any other features.

Giving tutorials and training

Unlike in an office, you can't gather your team around a computer as you show them how to do something. And if your team is distributed around the world with no common "wide awake and working" time, live screen sharing might not be the answer when it comes to training them up.

Enter… screen capture software! There are many different free and paid options, but here are my favourites:

Screencast-o-matic: www.worktravel.co/screencast

You can record up to 15 minutes of screen or webcam time for free, or you can pay $15 a year for no maximum recording time. You don't need to download or install anything on your computer either: just click "Start recording" and that's it.

If (like me) you tend to umm, ahhh and make a lot of mistakes when recording any sort of "how to" material, the $15-a-year option also provides editing tools.

ScreenFlow (for Mac users): www.worktravel.co/screenflow
Or Camtasia (for Windows users): www.worktravel.co/camtasia

Screencast-o-matic will suffice if you're giving the odd tutorial to your team, but if you really want to step things up a gear, you'll need to shell out some more money.

ScreenFlow and Camtasia allow you to layer video objects, images and audio clips over your main presentation – which means you could have a voiceover with a backing music track while a video plays of your presentation and there's a small square in the corner showing your face throughout. That sort of thing.

They're not cheap: ScreenFlow is $99 and Camtasia costs a whopping $299. Both offer a free trial before you commit.

Organisation

When a business consists of more than just you, it's easy to lose time to a big mess of where-do-I-find, how-do-I-do, what-the-eff-does-that-mean and whose-job-is-it-to among your staff.

And it's not even like you need a 50-strong team before you start having those issues: they appear as soon as you hire someone who isn't 100% privy to the workings of your brain. Just because *you* know how to do something or where a certain document is or what to do in a certain situation, it doesn't mean your staff do (or even your husband, as I've discovered on multiple occasions).

The key to all this, of course, is to remain organised and document everything – right from the start. While it's important for *all* businesses to be organised, it's particularly important for a distributed team: your employee can't walk up to your desk and ask you what happened when you last spoke to Mr Jones about his complaint "because he's on the phone right now and he doesn't seem very happy" – and you don't want them Skyping you either because it's 3am and you're asleep.

The next few pages discuss how we've learnt to stay organised within our company. It comes down to three things:

- Procedures
- Project management tools
- Cloud storage

Procedures

Right when we first started up Yellow Lettings – even before we had any staff – we decided that we wanted everything to be as procedure-driven as possible. And that means a LOT of "standard operating procedures" (SOPs).

We and our employees will create a procedure for *anything* that we'll need to do more than once – and that will benefit from being done the same way each time. For us, an obvious example is "Setting up a new tenancy" (when a person starts renting a house). This is a situation where it's vital that a long sequence of steps is completed: missing out a step could have pretty dire consequences. To save having to remember each step, we can just follow the SOP.

A less obvious example is "Starting your day". Opening the right pieces of software and completing the same few tasks isn't something a long-term member of staff is likely to forget. But if that person were to train someone else to take over from their role (temporarily or permanently), it would be much easier for everyone if it's all written down already.

Some people are against SOPs: they think that it removes all elements of creativity and autonomy from the workplace, resulting in a rigid working environment, miserable staff and a business that can't innovate. I get where they're coming from, but I disagree. In fact, in our company the opposite happens: by following procedures, we don't have to waste any mental energy on getting the ideal outcome every time – it just happens. We also get our work done more quickly because we don't forget things, have to correct mistakes, or ask someone what to do next. And all of this means that we can devote our mental energy to finding better ways to do things – trying new ideas that can be incorporated into new procedures if they're successful.

How our procedures are organised:

Until very recently, all our procedures were written up as Google Drive documents (www.worktravel.co/drive) in a dedicated "SOPs" folder. There was a "Master list of procedures" (a Google spreadsheet), which contained links to all the other procedures that had been written. The procedures covered everything – from "Tech setup for new starters" to "Referencing a tenant" and "Receiving an offer on a property".

And while Google Drive is more than adequate for SOPs, we'd reached the point where our procedure documents were becoming unwieldy: we just had too many, and they were too long, and people stopped bothering to update them (or even check them) because they were so hard to find and keep tidy.

So we've now moved on to some dedicated software called **Process Street** (www.worktravel.co/process). In Process Street, each procedure is a "workflow", and the workflows can be run through by different staff members as checklists – so we *know* they're being looked at and used. The software also keeps everything neat and organised, and the "drag and drop" feature makes it easy to switch around the order of a procedure.

You can also assign tasks to certain people, have conversations about tasks within the software itself, and do all manner of other things! We've only just started using it, but so far it's amazing.

Amazing and free! (Unless you want a few extra features, in which case it costs $5 per user per month.)

Whether you decide to use Google Drive, Process Street or anything else, one of the first procedures you create ought to be one called "Creating procedures": it should provide information about the structure of your SOPs, when to write them, how to write them, how/when to update them, different types of procedures, how to get them approved, and so on. The intention is that *anyone* can join your company and know exactly how to find SOPs that already exist, and create new ones or update existing ones if necessary.

What types of procedures might *your* business have? It really depends on what sort of business you run, but here are some random examples from different types of business:

- Write and publish a blog post.

- Add a new user to CRM software.

- Arrange and manage a meeting.

- Deal with a client complaint.

- Induct a new member of staff.

Now, you don't *have* to have SOPs if you don't want them or feel they're unnecessary for your business. All I'd say is this: if you decide to have them, get started on creating them right away. Because if you don't, you'll end up with a backlog of procedures that haven't been documented, and you almost certainly won't get around to creating them!

> While I can't share any of our new Process Street SOPs (because they're contained within password-protected software), I *can* share one of our Google Doc SOPs. **Register your purchase of this book at www.worktravel.co to see our SOP on "Setting up a job application form and collecting responses".**

Project management tools

A project management tool helps you plan and organise a project within your company. Many non-remote companies use them too – often when they're working with clients and contractors who aren't in the building (to keep them in the loop too), but even when they're working on purely in-house projects.

There are many project management tools out there with different (and overlapping) features, bells and whistles – so it's worth trying out a few before you commit. Some are cheap, and some cost a bloomin' fortune.

The key players at the time of writing are:

- Trello (www.worktravel.co/trello): completely free.

- Basecamp (www.worktravel.co/basecamp): from $20 a

month for up to ten active projects.

- Asana (www.worktravel.co/asana): completely free for up to 15 users, but there are also premium options.

- Teamwork (www.worktravel.co/teamwork): from $12 a month.

If you want to check out many more project management tools, head to Wikipedia's "Comparison of project management software" page: www.worktravel.co/pmtools.

Trello is our personal tool of choice – we use it to organise all the projects within our businesses and everything to do with our travel, too.

> For a case study of how we use Trello to organise one of our projects, register your purchase of this book at www.worktravel.co.

Cloud storage

Your employees are going to need to access, send and receive data from wherever they happen to be. And the easiest way to enable this is by using cloud storage.

(You could consider having a dedicated server, but it's hard to scale up or down with one: you'll need to fork out to rent/buy a lot of space that you don't know you'll ever make use of.)

So... cloud storage.

When you store your data "in the cloud", you're actually storing it with a service provider (like Dropbox or Google Drive) on their servers in a remote location. Whenever you make a change to your data – let's say you edit a document – that change is synced with the version that sits in the cloud, which in turn is synced with the version that sits on everyone's computers. Provided you have an internet connection, everyone's versions are constantly synced and up-to-date, which means that changes you make to a document will almost immediately be reflected in the same document sitting on your colleagues' computers.

The other benefit of cloud storage is that it acts as a handy backup. If your laptop gets stolen while you nip to the bathroom in a wifi cafe, it's not like you've lost all your data, because that data will have been synced to the cloud rather than be sitting on your computer alone. (You'll still have to fork out for a new laptop, of course, but at least you won't have to fork out for a new business.)

There are many cloud storage providers out there, with different price plans to suit different sizes of business and different types of need. Here are the most widely used:

- Dropbox: www.worktravel.co/dropbox

- OneDrive: www.worktravel.co/onedrive

- Google Drive: www.worktravel.co/drive

- Box: www.worktravel.co/box

- Amazon Cloud Drive: www.worktravel.co/acd

The prices and data allowances change constantly, so click on each link above to see the most up-to-date information.

Within our business we've chosen to go with Google Drive. It functions in exactly the same way as services like Dropbox for regular documents, but also allows you to create "Google Docs" – a special, collaborative type of document, spreadsheet or presentation.

Google Docs allow many people to edit them simultaneously – you can even see the edits happening in real time. This is great for frequently updated documents, because you don't get "version control" problems where two people simultaneously upload very slightly different versions of the same thing.

(A disadvantage of Google Docs used to be that they could only be viewed when connected to the internet, but an "offline mode" is now available: www.worktravel.co/docsoffline.)

Other useful tools and resources

Here's a grab bag of other nifty tools you might want to try out:

LastPass

Repetition alert! This was also mentioned in **Chapter 3: Guard Your Data.**

www.worktravel.co/lastpass

This password-management tool allows you to store all your super-strong and unguessable passwords in a vault so that you don't have to remember them – as indeed you *shouldn't* be able to remember your passwords. There's a brilliant extra benefit for businesses too though: if you need to share access to a particular site with a colleague or freelancer, LastPass will allow you to give them your login credentials *without revealing what they are* – and you can revoke access at any time.

LastPass is useful for all teams, but particularly distributed teams where you can't just shout across the office and ask for the password again.

LastPass is completely free to use on your computer. If you want to install the LastPass app on your smartphone, you'll need to purchase LastPass Premium, which costs $12 per year.

HelloSign

Repetition alert! This was also mentioned in **Chapter 5: Freelance From Anywhere.**

www.worktravel.co/hellosign

This cloud-based electronic signature tool allows users to sign, fill out, send, retrieve and save documents paperlessly – a lifesaver if you're always on the move and don't have easy access to a printer.

We use it all the time to sign documents: whenever we receive a PDF that we're supposed to download, print, sign, scan in and send back (pause for breath), we just sign it using a digital signature that we have stored on the site and send it back.

We also use it to get our clients and employees to sign stuff; they can either upload their signature like we have, or create a digital signature using a special tool on the website (don't worry: it's all legally binding).

Even if you need three people to sign the same document, HelloSign will email it to each of them and send reminders if they don't respond within a certain time.

HelloSign is free for unlimited self-signatures and up to three signature requests per month, then $15 per month. Check out the tour for a ton of nifty tips and integrations with other apps you use: www.worktravel.co/hellosigntour.

If you need to fill in complex forms with lots of fields (or you need other people to fill them in for you), take a look at EchoSign (www.worktravel.co/echosign): it costs $15 per month (there's no free plan), but it's a lot more sophisticated.

Mac user alert! You can also sign documents using Preview (although Preview doesn't have the extra features mentioned above).

Sqwiggle

www.worktravel.co/sqwiggle

OK so we don't use this ourselves, but plenty of distributed teams love it (including Buffer – see the interview with Buffer employee Carolyn Kopprasch in the **Appendix**). According to the website, it "makes it easy to create a fun and engaging company culture, even if your team is spread out across the world".

Here's how it works:

You're in a "Workroom" with fellow members of your company, and each person gets a personal photo in a grid of faces on your screen (think The Brady Bunch). Your photo gets updated a few times a minute: your webcam is actively taking photos of you.

To speak with anyone else in the Workroom, just click on their face. And that's it: you're connected – just like if you were in an office with them and turned your chair around to talk to them.

If you want to talk to more than one person, just click on more than one face and you'll be in group chat. Other team members can tell who's talking to whom by the matching coloured icons that appear next to each person's name – and if they want to join in, they can just click on a face.

Basically, Sqwiggle is permanently on in the background, passively taking snapshots of you and your colleagues. But you can become "active" within it at the click of a mouse – by clicking on another person's face and starting up a conversation.

Zapier

www.worktravel.co/zapier

Zapier "connects the web apps you use to easily move your data and automate tedious tasks", according to its website. And it really does just that!

To explain how it works, here's an example of a "Zap":

When I receive a new email in Gmail, send me an SMS message.

The first part (receiving a new email) is the trigger. The second part (sending an SMS message) is the action. Together they form the Zap.

Here are some more examples:

- *When I get a new entry from a Wufoo form, create a new lead in Salesforce.*

- *When I label an email in Gmail, subscribe them to a MailChimp mailing list.*

- *When a new file is added to Google Drive, copy it to Dropbox.*

- *When a Google Calendar event is taking place tomorrow, send a Slack notification.*

Zapier supports over 500 apps – many of which you probably already use – and they work together in ingenious ways. You can check them all out here: www.worktravel.co/zapbook.

(There's a similar service called IFTTT – If This Then That: www.worktravel.co/ifttt. It offers fewer integrations than Zapier but it's free, so you should take a look there first and see if it suits your needs.)

> **If you register your purchase of this book at www.worktravel.co, you'll get to see how we make use of Zapier when hiring:** just head to the SOP called "Setting up a job application form and collecting responses".

Conclusion

I've chucked a heckuva lot of URLs and logistics-related information your way, and you might be feeling a bit overwhelmed. It's important to remember that you won't necessarily need *all* these tools and ideas – you can just start with the ones that meet your business's most pressing needs right now, and then consider trying out some of the others if and when you decide you need them.

To find out how other businesses are run (and the tools and techniques they use), head to the **Appendix** for interviews with different types of digital nomad.

*Note: if your business has clients and you'd like more information about cross-currency payments, there's a section in **Chapter 5: Freelance From Anywhere** called "Getting paid as a digital nomad freelancer". The advice there could come in useful for you too.*

Bonus Chapter: Travel Like A Pro

This book is about getting to grips with all the "on the ground" stuff associated with working while you travel. If you want to absolutely nail the prep and planning process of travel, you need my *other* book, Travel Like A Pro (www.worktravel.co/protravel)!

This bonus chapter contains some of my favourite tips from the book.

Discover the best-value flights

While I've yet to find a failsafe five-minute strategy for getting the best-value flights, I *have* found an assortment of useful websites and tools that help me reach that goal. It's not the most elegant approach, but it works.

None of my methods involve stitching multiple flights together to reach your destination, or flying somewhere and then hiring a car to drive the final 200-odd miles. I figure you've got better things to do with your time.

Start with Skyscanner

Skyscanner (www.worktravel.co/skyscanner) is a price-comparison and booking site for both domestic and international flights. It searches through "thousands of websites to find you the very best travel deals" across the majority of airlines, and presents them to you in price order.

When you find a deal you want, you can click to be connected to the airline or travel agent to make your booking directly with them. Skyscanner doesn't charge a fee for this (the airline or travel agent pays them a small referral fee instead), so you don't need to worry about paying extra.

There are lots of Skyscanner-esque sites out there, but I like this one because of the flexible search options: you can browse prices across an entire month or year, so – if your dates are flexible – you can make sure you're getting the best rates possible. It's also very user-friendly.

Here's what to do once you're on Skyscanner:

1. Enter your starting city and destination, and search to find the best flights for you. **If your dates are flexible, look at the "month" or "year" view to see the best days to fly.** (Alternatively, search for specific dates and once you're in the results page, click the right or left arrow to move up or down a day and see if the price changes.)

2. Once you're on the results screen, make a note of the best prices for the most suitable flights for you – and the airlines they're with. (You might be able to find a better deal out there if you do some more searching, which is why it's best not to book right away.)

If you're not a fan of Skyscanner or want to try something else, here are some other sites that aggregate airfares and allow you to book through them:

- Google Flights Explorer: www.worktravel.co/gfe

- Kayak: www.worktravel.co/kayak

- Hipmunk: www.worktravel.co/hipmunk

Look up low-cost airlines separately

Southwest and Virgin America don't appear in Skyscanner's fare listings, and there are a few other airlines (like JetBlue) that don't appear on other aggregator sites. There might be a direct flight with one of those airlines, so check to see if that's the case.

Here's a Wikipedia list of all the low-cost airlines: www.worktravel.co/lowcost.

And this site will give you a list of routes from low-cost airlines if you enter your starting location and final destination (Europe only): www.worktravel.co/lowcostguide.

Check for hidden fees

We once booked a crack-of-dawn Ryanair flight from a middle-of-nowhere airport because we thought the fare was far cheaper than the airline offering the next best fare: British Airways. But after accounting for baggage fees (we had check-in bags at the time), the extra charge for reserving seats, and the time and cost of travelling to the middle-of-nowhere airport, we'd have been far better off going with BA (and we'd have had a lot more sleep).

Before you book anything, check for all the hidden fees! And if you value your time, make sure you account for that too.

- **SeatGuru (www.worktravel.co/seatguru) has lists of all the baggage prices for each individual airline, as well as fees for checking in** – click on "Browse Airlines" at the top of the page. Bear in mind that SeatGuru's information is sometimes out of date, so you should check the airline's website too – once you've narrowed down your flight options.

- **Use Google Maps (www.worktravel.co/gmaps) to see where the airport is in relation to your starting or destination city,** and – once the airport appears on the screen – use "Directions" to find out how long it'll take by different types of transit. If it turns out you can only get to the airport by taxi, Google "taxi fare calculator [name of city]": at least one website should appear in the search results to help you figure out an approximate price.

Check the airline's site directly for deals

Airlines often have deals that aren't advertised on price-comparison/aggregator sites, so – once you know what flights are available – you could quickly check the deals page of any relevant airlines to see if discounts are available.

Track flights for price drops

Yapta (www.worktravel.co/yapta) is my hero website. It will track flight prices for you and alert you (by email, text, or through its iPhone app) whenever the price drops below a level you specify. You can then pounce as soon as the price is something you're comfortable with.

Don't stop once you've booked the flight! If the fare falls below what you paid for your ticket within 24 hours of your purchase, many airlines will refund you without penalty and allow you to rebook at the lower price. Use Yapta to track the flight you booked and alert you if it falls below what you paid. Yapta can then walk you through what to do to collect your refund. Find out more here: www.worktravel.co/yaptarefunds.

Once your 24-hour window is up, Yapta can also email you if the airfare drops by more than the cost of the airline's change fee (the fee that kicks in for non-flexible tickets after 24 hours). You can then rebook at the lower price, pay the change fee and pocket the difference. More here: www.worktravel.co/yaptarefunds.

If you have niche travel requirements...

If the price is right but you're *not quite ready* to book: use Options Away (www.worktravel.co/optionsaway) to hold today's price for up to 14 days (for a small fee). If the airfare drops, you pay the lower price. If you decide not to travel, do nothing and let your hold expire. (At the moment, Options Away covers US domestic flights only.)

If you have a complex, multi-leg route: Orbitz (www.worktravel.co/orbitz) is the most user-friendly when it comes to "multi-city" trips.

Extra tips

A few more tidbits of advice:

- **Try buying flights as if you're from another country.** For example, if you're American and you're flying from Sydney to Bangkok, search for prices on the Australian and Thai versions of the airline's site, rather than the US one: you can sometimes get better prices this way (but ensure that the charges levied on foreign currency transactions by your bank/credit card company doesn't screw up any savings).

- **Within 24 hours of booking a flight, check to see if the price has fallen.** If it has, you can usually get a full refund and rebook at the lower price. See the previous section of how you can use Yapta to track price changes on your behalf.

- **Waiting until the last minute to book is a risky move.** Most of the time, the fare will increase rapidly just before a flight, because it's filling up with other people and you're clearly desperate. On routes with significant competition though – like LA to New York – you might get lucky: some airlines will have sales if they're not selling enough seats quickly enough.

- It's probably best not to pay attention to a lot of the myths/no-longer-true situations about booking flights...

    - **Tuesday afternoon (or Wednesday morning, or Thursday evening) isn't the best time to search for flights, and the weekend isn't the worst time.** New fares are filed electronically – and they're filed throughout the day using a dedicated system that calculates how many seats are left on any given flight (unlike the old days when staff would manually enter new fares in batches).

    - **Websites aren't sneakily tracking how often you check a flight and upping the price because they can tell you're interested.** This myth was all over the internet a while back, and people were encouraged to use an incognito browser when viewing fares so that airline and flight-aggregator websites couldn't keep tabs on them. The myth was corroborated by the fact that people *would* often see two different fares for the same flight if they switched between their regular browser window and an incognito one.

But as Hipmunk explains, "What might be happening is that, if you get as far as the booking step for a ticket and it's the last seat at that price, the airline will put it 'on hold' until you've finished your purchase. So if you do another flight search immediately after, without releasing that seat, you might see tickets starting at the next price level." It's not in the interests of the website to raise the price, because you might go off looking for the cheaper price you'd seen earlier. (www.worktravel.co/myth1)

- **You won't get the cheapest fare by booking a year – or even a few months – in advance.** As Bill Brunger, former vice president of Continental Airlines, explains, "[The airlines} don't know too much" a year out. "When revenue management people are nervous they usually pick a default level that's conservative." (Source: www.worktravel.co/myth2) When *is* the best time? Well… it very much depends on the time of year and destination, so your best bet is to start tracking your flights ASAP (see the previous section on Yapta price alerts) and choose to buy when the price is something you're comfortable with.

If you're still keen on *some* kind of guidance for when to book flights… this Reddit thread shows the progression of ticket prices from two weeks to four months prior to departure date, and it suggests that between four and eight weeks before departure is a good time to book: www.worktravel.co/whentobook1. And this study shows that prices start dropping at the three-month mark, with the cheapest tickets ranging from three weeks to ten weeks in advance: www.worktravel.co/whentobook2.

Choose the best seats on your flight

Most airlines will allow you to choose your seats (although the low-cost airlines will often charge a fee for doing so). But beyond knowing whether you're an aisle kinda guy or a window-obsessed gal, how do you decide which part of the plane to pick?

(If you've never thought or worried about this before, ignore this section and go on as you were. There's no point in *adding* to your list of frustrations and worries when it comes to flying.)

SeatGuru (www.worktravel.co/seatguru) is both your match made in heaven and your potential rabbit hole: there's just way too much fun to be had with airline-related information. SeatGuru has seating maps for all airlines, but where things get *really* cool is that the maps are colour-coded according to how good the seats are: some are considered superior according to the price you paid, while others are marked as downright awful and not worth a penny.

And who decides on the "colours" of the seats? Anyone – including you! The information is crowdsourced by users of the site. You'll also see a few written reviews of seats next to each plane's seating map.

(If you want to waste the rest of your day on airplane-related geekery, head to SeatGuru to compare all the airlines' first class cabins: www.worktravel.co/firstclass. You can also browse SeatGuru's ever-fascinating blog: www.worktravel.co/sgblog.)

Frequent flyer deals

In frequent flyer land, everything's constantly in flux. From the best deals to the best cards to the best hacks… it all changes practically daily. For that reason, it's way more useful to check out constantly updated websites on the matter rather than a book – so I'm providing you with some great links to get you started.

If you're a US resident…

If you're a US resident or have managed to apply for US credit cards, you're one of the lucky ones: frequent flyer miles are far more generous – and there's far more information about them – in the US than anywhere else in the world.

Getting started

- Start by reading this beginner's guide to miles and points from **Million Mile Secrets:** www.worktravel.co/mms-guide. It's thoroughly comprehensive and will tell you everything you could possibly want to know.

If you'd like to do a bit more reading around the subject from a few different sources though, here are some other recommendations:

- Cards For Travel has a great step-by-step guide to understanding frequent flyer miles and getting started: www.worktravel.co/cft-guide.

- You should also read this FAQ from them, because it's ace: www.worktravel.co/cft-faq.

- Travis from Extra Pack of Peanuts has a comprehensive and thoroughly useful article called "How to use frequent flyer miles: the mega FAQ": www.worktravel.co/epp-faq.

- Also be sure to read his "Six myths of frequent flyer miles": www.worktravel.co/epp-myths.

Finding the best deals

You only really need to check out one or two blogs for the best deals, because they'll usually tell you the same thing. Here are a few constantly updated sites:

- The Points Guy: www.worktravel.co/tpg-deals

- Million Mile Secrets: www.worktravel.co/mms-deals

- Extra Pack of Peanuts: www.worktravel.co/epp-deals

You could also look at some forums. FlyerTalk is a popular one: www.worktravel.co/ft-deals.

If you're from the rest of the world...

Sorry to bunch you together with everyone else in the non-American world! It's just that there really isn't much in the way of information – because the perks are less widely available (and less good).

Take a quick look at the links in the previous section for US residents, because some of that information (especially the introductory guides) will still be relevant to you.

Here are some extra links to check out:

- If you're a UK resident, **MoneySavingExpert** is the place to go for a full explanation of how it all works, as well as up-to-date deals: www.worktravel.co/mse-guide.

- If you're Australian, **Point Hacks** is a great resource for information and deals: www.worktravel.co/pointhacks.

- Canadian? Head on over to **Rewards Canada** for step-by-step instructions to choosing a card, and links to the best deals: www.worktravel.co/rewardscanada. There's also a great blog called Canadian Kilometers, which is all about frequent flyer miles (or kilometers) from a

Canadian perspective: www.worktravel.co/canadiankm.

There are also some great message boards and forums about frequent flyer programs. **FlyerTalk** comes highly recommended: www.worktravel.co/ft-deals (scroll down to the bottom for discussions on European, Asian, Australian, etc. airlines).

Insurance

There are two kinds of insurance you need to be aware of when you travel: travel insurance and expat health insurance.

Travel insurance

Think of travel insurance as cover for emergencies - for situations when your bags get stolen, you have to cancel your trip at the last moment, or you get eaten by a panda. Travel insurance is essentially for the big bad stuff that's unlikely to happen but might.

Most travel insurance products are aimed at people who take the odd vacation, and they stipulate the following:

- You need to be in your home country at the time of purchasing the insurance.

- When you take out the insurance, you usually need to specify a return date (or at the very least, your insurance will expire after a certain number of months and you'll have to return home).

- You can't renew the insurance while on the move.

Luckily, more and more travel insurance options are coming onto the market for people who travel long-term and have no return date - meaning you often *don't* need to be in your home country at the time of purchasing the insurance, you *don't* need to specify a return date, and you *can* renew the insurance while on the move.

Here are a few companies that come highly recommended; check them all out because some might be more reasonably priced than others depending on where you're from and where you're travelling:

- **World Nomads** (www.worktravel.co/worldnomads) is a firm favourite among digital nomads. The staff are known to be friendly and helpful on the phone, and they're also great at answering questions on Twitter (@WorldNomads). They provide a lot of coverage and - according to many - will process claims quickly and fairly rather than try to find ways to get out of them.

- **Worldwide Insure offers "Longstay Travel Insurance"** (www.worktravel.co/worldinsure) for EU residents. Areas of travel can be mixed to suit your needs, and you can extend the travel insurance any number of times while you're still travelling.

- **World Escapade** (www.worktravel.co/escapade) gives you the option to *just* have medical coverage and none of the other stuff (like cancellation and baggage coverage), which is a great idea.

Expat health insurance

Think of expat health insurance as your replacement for the regular healthcare you get (or used to get) in your home country. If you're American, think of it as health insurance. If you're British, think of it as the NHS or private healthcare.

Whereas travel insurance covers you for medical emergencies, expat health insurance is there for your dental check-ups, your earache, your flu-like symptoms and - with certain provisos - your pregnancy.

You don't just have to live in one country as an expat - you can buy insurance that will cover you for medical attention all over the world.

To find the best expat health insurance for your needs, there's no need to trawl through all the different health insurance sites. Instead, just head to **Broker Fish** (www.worktravel.co/brokerfish).

It's pretty nifty: it allows you to compare all the expat health insurance plans easily, and you have lots of options for filtering down your results. For example, you can choose what types of cover you want (dental, out-patient, well-being, etc.), how much you want your deductible to be (the higher the deductible, the lower the monthly premium - and vice versa), where in the world you want to be covered, and so on.

There's no charge for using Broker Fish: the company receives commission from any insurer it places cover with instead. And because there's relatively little variation in the amount that Broker Fish receives by plan or insurer, there's no reason for them to recommend one over another to you.

There's SO much more to insurance!

This section gives you the "need to know" information, but if you want to better understand all your options (and what you do and don't get with your insurance), you'll be wanting to read my other book, Travel Like A Pro (www.worktravel.co/protravel).

Visas

We digital nomads are in a bit of a grey area when it comes to visas – the main reason being that the reality of being able to work online has overtaken the rules that govern international work.

Working visas are intended for people who are working for employers (and potentially taking jobs away from locals) in the area, and business visas are for those who are there purely to further their business in some way. Digital nomads don't fall into either category, so the majority of us tend to imagine ourselves as tourists – because there aren't really any other options for us.

What does this mean in practice?

- If tourists need a visa to enter a particular country (e.g. Thailand, if staying longer than 30 days), digital nomads will get a tourist visa – and if any border officials ask, they're there for a vacation.

- If tourists don't need a visa to enter a particular country (e.g. Hong Kong), digital nomads won't get any sort of visa.

You can use VisaHQ to find out if tourist visas are required for the country you're planning to visit: www.worktravel.co/visahq.

If you're happy to take the "I'm a tourist" approach to visas and you find out you *do* need a tourist visa for your destination, your next step is to search online for information about whether you can get one on arrival or if you should order it in advance. (If you're required to order it in advance, you'll need to send off your passport to the relevant embassy and wait a while – so try to get on top of it as soon as possible!)

In some countries, you're allowed to renew your tourist visa at least once while you're still in the country. In other countries, you have to leave and come back again. Google "visa run [country]" for more information and advice.

Do you need a visa for your layover?

If you're flying into one country's airport simply to fly straight out to another destination, you may still need a visa for that intermediary country - even if you don't ever leave the airport.

The rules vary widely, so you'll need to do some Googling: search for "transit visa [country of layover]" and some useful results should appear.

Even if you don't need a visa, you can't stay forever!

While many countries will let you into the country visa-free, there's still usually a maximum number of days you can stay in that country. For example, if you're American you'll be allowed into Germany without a visa… but you're allowed there for a maximum of 90 days out of every 180 days.

If you want to stay longer than your allowance, you may have to apply for some sort of visa or residency - it will depend on where you're going.

Occasionally there are nifty workarounds - especially when it comes to living in Europe. If you're not European and you want to stay there for longer than 90 days, Nomadic Matt has some ideas on how to achieve it: www.worktravel.co/90days.

Airport and flight survival tips

"Staying organised" isn't just about arriving at the airport on time and having your passport with you. If you want to be a travel ninja (and avoid all the fluster and panic that goes with *not* being one) read on…

- **Set a calendar reminder to check in online.** Some airlines allow you to check in up to a month before your flight – which seems insane but there you go. Other airlines will allow you to check in 24 hours before your flight. And certain flights don't really "do" check in anymore. For example, when you buy certain tickets with Vueling, you automatically check in at the same time.

- **Check in online.** If you don't already check in online, you're a) missing a trick and b) errr… insane?? Checking in online means the following:

    - You don't have to check in at the airport, which is SO much quicker (especially if you're travelling with carry-on only and can proceed straight to security).

    - Most of the time, you can get your boarding pass sent to your smartphone after you've checked in online – meaning you don't have to locate an internet cafe to print it out before the flight (and it's one less thing to remember to take to the airport).

    - With some airlines, you can only choose your seats during the check-in process (not before). If you wait until you reach the airport to check in, you might miss out on all the best seats.

    - Remember: some airlines ONLY let you check in online!

- **Assume you'll be caught in a traffic jam** (or insane train delays) on your way to the airport – i.e. leave for the airport *really* early! It's better for your nerves, and you can use the extra time at the airport to listen to podcasts, read a book, or do some work.

- **Always have *one* place where you keep your passport and boarding pass** (if it isn't an electronic one), so that you always know where they are. They should be easy to retrieve at the airport, because you'll need to pull them out every five bloomin' seconds.

- **Wear clothes that don't need a belt.** Wear shoes that can be slipped on and off easily. And if at all possible, pack your jacket in your carry-on. It all leads to less hassle in the security line.

- **Put your liquids, laptop and other electronic devices in a place that's really easy to reach within your bag.** Again – for ease at security.

- **Make sure your laptop and other electronic items are fully charged.** (In certain countries you might be asked to switch on your device, and if you can't (because the batteries are dead), you won't be allowed to take it on the flight – and there's a good chance you won't be allowed on the flight either. Turning on an electronic device can show a security screener that the batteries aren't in fact hidden explosives.

- **Buy a retractable cable lock for your bag.** While you're in the departure area, use it to lock the zippers together and then tie the bag to a permanent structure. I use the Pacsafe lock, which is widely available: www.worktravel.co/lock. Plenty of other brands do them too.

- **Take an empty water bottle with you through security**, so that you don't have to pay the always-exorbitant price for a bottle of water in the departure area.

- **Have enough cash with you to buy anything you might need at the airport.** Some airports (I'm looking at you, Sofia-Vrazhdebna Airport) don't have ATMs, and their stores don't take cards.

- **Take food with you for the flight.** It's cheaper, healthier and tastier. You're allowed to take your own food through security, unless it's in liquid form (like yoghurt) – then it's subject to the same rules as other liquids in your carry-on baggage.

(Bear in mind that for some reason you're NOT allowed to take outside food onboard an AirAsia flight. But everyone does anyway, and no one seems to get into trouble for it.)

- **Listen/look out for your gate announcement** and don't dilly-dally when you hear/see it. And consider buying a Speedy Boarding ticket for low-cost airlines. Essentially, you want to be on the plane putting your bag in its overhead compartment ASAP.

- **Keep a pen handy for writing out your landing card/ customs form** on the plane.

Conclusion

A while ago I met up with a reader when we were both living in Valencia. He asked me if I was happier since quitting my job and becoming a digital nomad. Rather than start yabbering away – which I normally do because I hate silences – I actually took a moment to think about it.

No. I'm not happier.

If Rob and I had never discovered this lifestyle, we'd be absolutely fine – and I'd be just as happy as I am today.

I'm not any happier, but I'm more fulfilled. I get to do work I love alongside the person I love, from wherever we want to live. We've founded a business that doesn't shackle us to an office or particular way of doing things. We're free to make our own decisions on almost everything – which means we've made a fair few mistakes along the way and had to learn from them, fast.

Sometimes, we're probably more stressed than we'd be if we had a more "traditional" life: 2am team meetings and crappy Thai wifi are going to do that to you.

But *never* do we feel like jacking it all in for 9-to-5 employment.

Because the sense of freedom and fulfilment is overwhelming. It's addictive. And it's SO much better than just "happiness".

This lifestyle isn't necessarily "easy" – and I hope this book has helped to explain the sort of preparation and thought that needs to go into it.

It isn't easy, but it's incredible.

Appendix: Interviews

This appendix is divided into two parts.

The first part contains interviews with lots of different digital nomads – people who do very different types of work and have a variety of travel habits. There's no "right way" to do this whole digital nomad thing – and you definitely don't have to be a programmer, designer or writer to make it work. Not anymore, anyway.

The second part contains some interviews with *parents* who travel while they work. The one thing I can't speak with any authority on is how to do all this with children – so I've asked some people with a wealth of experience to help me out and answer a bunch of questions relating to practicalities, logistics, socialising and education.

Mish Slade 216

Part 1: Different types of digital nomad

Andres Zuleta: Founder and CEO 218

Carolyn Kopprasch: Remote employee at Buffer 224

Crystal Bryant: Developer and writer 235

Mark Gibson: Circus school owner & remote worker .. 240

Lewis Smith: Freelance developer & app creator 245

Blake Boles: Adventure company owner 251

Kathryn O'Halloran: Romance fiction writer 259

Pete Domican: Remote management consultant 274

Eli Trier: Artist, author & illustrator 280

Jewels Velky: Photographer & consultant 283

Adam & Lindsey Nubern: Accountant & consultant .. 288

Jennifer Harris: Software company owner 298

Johanna Read: freelance writer & photographer 303

Andres Zuleta: Founder and CEO

Tell us a bit about you and what you do – both in terms of your work and travel habits.

I run Boutique Japan (www.boutiquejapan.com) – a bespoke travel service for enthusiastic travelers. We specialize in private cultural and culinary trips for savvy travelers from the US, Australia, and around the world.

Boutique Japan is a location-independent business in almost every way, but we're technically based in California, USA. At the moment I'm living in San Diego (where I have lived for most of the past few years), but I have run this business while traveling around the world, including long (multi-month) stays in Japan, Mexico and Thailand, and short stays in several other countries.

Generally I travel with my partner, Christina, although on occasion I attend conferences and meetups on my own. The business doesn't require me to be in any one place, and all our systems are set up to function from anywhere with an internet connection.

What did you do before you set up Boutique Japan?

My last job before embarking on entrepreneurship was at a travel company, where I discovered that I really enjoyed this type of sales.

I'd never, ever considered myself a salesperson, and before working in the travel industry didn't have any sales experience, per se. But I discovered that I enjoyed speaking with people about their desired travel plans, researching interesting destinations around the world, and helping people coordinate their dream trips.

Eventually I decided to focus exclusively on the country in which I had the deepest interest: Japan. Having lived there for several years – and finding that, even after moving back to the US, I couldn't get rid of the persistent desire to keep visiting to eat and explore – Japan unexpectedly became a lifelong passion.

What steps did you take to transition towards becoming location independent?

The first step was coming up with a viable business idea. This was the hardest part for me. I spent the better part of two years reading business books, listening to podcasts, brainstorming, and trying things out before I finally thought of one that stuck.

The next step was convincing myself that I could do it. I wasn't born feeling like an entrepreneur, so it took a while for the idea to sink in. I joined a couple of online business forums, where I had the chance to chat and exchange ideas and feedback with fellow entrepreneurs and wantrepreneurs, and this was invaluable.

Next came discussing the idea with my partner, Christina. It wasn't a very hard sell, because she's also passionate about travel. But she wasn't always keen on the idea of selling everything and traveling the world indefinitely, so there were many heart-to-heart conversations.

Setting up the business itself took a great deal of work, and from the start I actively set things up to work remotely, because I knew I wanted to travel a lot. This meant, for example, finding fax software, rather than buying a fax machine; and setting up virtual phone networks, rather than investing in fancy office phones. These are just two small examples, of course.

Then we sold everything. This was an amazing moment, and even as relative minimalists we realized how much we had. We finally whittled everything down to a couple of suitcases, and about one box each to keep at a relative's house in San Diego.

Finally, we decided where to begin (Japan) and bought our tickets. The rest is history.

Do you hire employees or contractors?

We hire outside experts for a lot of individual things (the usual: accounting, bookkeeping, legal, etc.) but don't have any employees right now.

We had a virtual assistant (VA) in the past, but she was only with us for six months. We're hiring again soon (in the next couple of months), now that we have a better idea of what we're doing, and how to create a position (and manage).

Our VA was based in Asia, and our next employee will be remote, but we don't know yet where they will be from – could be US, Australia, Japan, or elsewhere in the world!

This will be a full-time employee, and we plan to use our own website to find them, though may also post the job elsewhere.

How does your business find new clients?

Primarily thanks to content marketing, focused around our blog. Our business is under two years old, but we're starting to receive referrals as well.

What was your main reason for wanting to live this sort of lifestyle?

Freedom and adventure.

I love travel, and the idea of quitting my job and traveling the world – while working on my own business – seemed irresistibly appealing. Even now as I write those words, I wonder how anyone can resist.

How do you stay productive?

I can't help but want to work – especially as we continue to build and develop our business – but taking regular breaks is essential in order to maintain perspective and focus on the right tasks (i.e. those that will have the most impact for us and our clients).

What does a typical day look like for you?

I usually start working around 8am or so.

My day consists of speaking with potential new clients, corresponding with current clients whose trips are coming up, and working on a variety of others tasks – from writing blogs and newsletters, to trying to devise new systems to increase our efficiency.

I've found that I work best in about two or three-hour blocks, interspersed with breaks, though I don't always stick to this as I probably should.

I generally stop being very productive sometime in the mid-afternoon, when I am best served by taking an extended break.

When in the US or elsewhere in the Americas, I usually correspond with contacts based in Japan in the evening for a little while.

What do you wish you'd known at the start?

Taking your laptop to the beach is stupid.

That being said, those cliché digital nomad photos of laptops in paradise did spur me to attain the lifestyle they promise, so I think they definitely serve a purpose.

What's the hardest thing about being location independent?

I have no complaints – being able to work from anywhere beats not having the freedom to move around.

What tools, equipment or tactics do you rely on for travelling while working?

Asana (www.worktravel.co/asana) for project management, almost anything by Google (docs, calendars, etc.), Slack (www.worktravel.co/slack) for team chat, Toggle (www.worktravel.co/toggl) for time-tracking, and coffee.

Carolyn Kopprasch: Remote employee at Buffer

Can you explain a bit about what Buffer is, and the "distributed team" nature of it? Did the founders proactively set out to create a distributed company, or did things just happen that way?

Sure! Buffer (www.bufferapp.com) is a software company, and we've made the decision to be completely remote. That is, absolutely anyone can be absolutely anywhere, regardless of team, role, project, etc.

I love that you asked this, because no, originally, we thought we'd all end up in San Francisco together. Joel, our founder and CEO, made the decision to be fully remote after a lot of advice from and discussion with Leo, his cofounder, the rest of the team, and other founders.

He (we) decided that living *now* is too important, and doing whatever will make you the happiest shouldn't be delayed.

He wrote two amazing blog posts about this decision process:

- "Questions I ask myself about working as a distributed team": www.worktravel.co/buffer1

- "The joys and benefits of working as a distributed team": www.worktravel.co/buffer2

What's your role at Buffer – and what sort of work do you do on a daily basis?

My official title is Chief Happiness Officer, although we adjust and change our roles and tasks a lot based on needs and our current experiments. In short, I help with the "Happiness Team," which is the customer service team at Buffer. I do hiring, coaching current team members, working on improving our customer experience, and of course, answering customer emails and tweets.

- "On leadership and titles at Buffer":

www.worktravel.co/buffer3

- "A day in the life of a Buffer Happiness Hero": www.worktravel.co/buffer4

How did you apply for and get the job at Buffer? And what was it about the company that made you want to work there?

I was already a customer, and a fan of the team and their product.

The first inkling that I might want to look closely at Buffer came when I emailed a support question a few months after becoming a customer. I received the most caring, delightful and helpful email I'd seen in a long time. I had a similar experience a few months later. I knew that a company that cared that much about its customers was one I wanted to keep an eye on and learn from.

I had been extremely happy at my job in Nashville, TN, but simply couldn't resist the call for Happiness Heroes based in the US. (Joel and Leo were in Tel Aviv at the time.) I applied for the job in September of 2012.

They kindly interviewed me on a weekend so that I wouldn't have to leave work, and when they arrived at their offices at the interview time, they realized that it was locked for the weekend. Rather than reschedule me, they stood on the sidewalk and picked up the office wifi and interviewed me together, right there, one headphone each. I loved them instantly. At the end of the chat, they asked if I could start immediately, and so I spent the next few hours (and nights and weekends for the next 2 weeks while I finished up my other job) answering customer emails. It's a great memory. Nothing screamed "start up" to me like interviewing me on the street and then getting set up to help out that day.

What sort of person do you need to be if you want to work well in a distributed team?

This is a toughie! To be completely honest, I don't think that you have to *be* anything in order to work well in a distributed team. I think there are some things that you have to *learn to be*, which is an important distinction.

I wasn't a natural at remote work at first. I went a bit crazy with the lack of interpersonal interaction in the first few weeks. (We now have tons of video chats but in those days we didn't. We might have one video chat a day, and without any roommates or pets, I sometimes didn't speak unless I went out of the house. I quickly became a regular at the local coffee shops! All that to say, I think anyone can work on and learn to be a great, happy, productive remote worker.

Anyway... I do think that in order to be in a distributed team, you have to be willing to put a lot of energy into your communication. It's not that only one communication style can work. But regardless of what medium, and how often, and what style, I think you have to be willing to make it a top priority. It helps to be willing to communicate about your communication, too. We have regular-ish meta meetings, where we'll reflect on what we feel is and isn't working about our communication.

(I truly believe that someday I'll be well set up for a ridiculously successful (or perhaps nauseatingly self-examining) romantic relationship by practicing these conversations!)

How do you feel your relationships with your colleagues differs from if you were all in the same office together?

I love this question, because we've thought a ton about this.

Because we can't rely on the usual bonding practices of colleagues like softball teams, drinks after work, office kitchen run-ins, and the like, we've had to be extremely intentional about how we connect as friends and colleagues.

We have tried to set up a culture where our value of self-improvement is one of the central sources of connection.

It's because of this that we've revolved a lot of our "perks" around this value. That is, we offer our teammates a Kindle, unlimited Kindle books, a Jawbone Up (for each teammate, and partners), and others in the same vein. This helps us work on our own self-improvement (through reading, better sleep and more exercise), but it also provides a way to connect with other teammates when you don't have the usual small talk.

I was surprised to see this unfold, but I'd say that we're close in a unique way. In some ways, I think we're close in ways that are a lot more powerful than if we were in the same office, and perhaps would even be difficult to achieve if we had the proximity to fall back on.

- The ten Buffer values: www.worktravel.co/buffer5

Are you free to travel as much as you like while you work?

Yup! Of course, we use good judgement, prioritize productivity, minimize inconveniences for colleagues, and try to always ensure that we have great wifi. And we live and learn!

- "From Taiwan to Bali: How I toured Asia, while working as an engineer for a distributed team": www.worktravel.co/buffer6

- "5 continents, 14 cities, 24 people: how we work as a distributed team spread across the planet": www.worktravel.co/buffer7

Do you have any tips or hacks for staying productive while moving to new destinations?

Oh, lots! I was just in Venice, Italy for a month. I learned to say the word "unlimited" when discussing wifi with Airbnb hosts or other accommodation. I'm spoiled by never learning that lesson the hard way until leaving the US!

The other one that comes to mind is: set up all of your 2-factor authentication* either though Authy (www.worktravel.co/authy), Google Authenticator (www.worktravel.co/authenticator), or with a Google Voice (www.worktravel.co/voice) (or similar) phone number. I had my US phone number saved for 2-factor auth for a few sites, and that slowed me down a bit while traveling. Good lesson to learn!

- "How I learned to balance work, family, and life through remote work": www.worktravel.co/buffer8

- The highs and lows of 11 cities in 3 months: www.worktravel.co/buffer9

[Two-factor authentication is a simple security feature that requires both "something you know" (like a password) and "something you have" (like your phone). For example, if you enable two-factor authentication on your Google account, you'll have to enter your password as usual, and then you'll be asked for a verification code that will be sent to your phone via text, voice call, or the Google mobile app. If a hacker has your laptop and is trying to get into your account, they can't unless they have your phone too. My other book, Protect Your Tech, discusses it in more detail: www.worktravel.co/protectyourtech.]

What methods/processes does Buffer use to hire people who will be a great fit for the company?

Our best hack here is that we only hire our customers! We ask people to use the product and get to know the company for 3 months before applying. This may cause us to lose the chance to talk to some talented people, but it also helps us ensure that the people we talk to already "get it" and are excited about our unique approach.

- "How we hire at Buffer": www.worktravel.co/buffer10

Buffer is known for being a very "transparent" company – not just in terms of revealing revenue figures and publishing how

much everyone earns, but also when it comes to health and wellbeing among employees. Can you explain more about that? And do you think it's something all distributed companies need to embrace?

No, I don't think that all distributed companies need to embrace this. We've chosen "Have a focus on self-improvement" as one of our keystone values, so it makes a lot of sense for us to support that goal. Transparency is another keystone value, and sharing our self-improvement efforts (and goals and successes and failures) helps us connect with each other about these topics.

I think it's great, and I believe that any individual person at any company (distributed or local) could embrace this and find others who feel the same. I don't feel that all companies *should*, however. It is so powerful and so celebrated because it is a direct result of the values we've chosen and reflect who we are anyway.

What tools and strategies does Buffer use to ensure that everyone at the company remains happy, motivated, effective, and part of a team?

We've constantly adjusting this, so here's how it is this moment:

- We have a daily pair call with another member of the Buffer team. This rotates every week. We talk about what we're working on at Buffer, and what we're working on in our self-improvement.

- We have weekly "masterminds" with a peer, where we

discuss challenges and celebrate achievements.

- We have weekly "1:1s" with mentors, to set and plan for higher-level goals, explore challenges from another perspective, and generally question anything and everything to improve as much (and as constantly) as possible.

- And we have periodic Buffer retreats in places like Bangkok, Cape Town, Sydney, New York and Reykjavic to work together for a week and play together on the weekends.

How about logistics: how are time differences, meetings, communication in general, etc. managed?

This one constantly changes too! We have a lot of communication options and we try to choose our medium carefully. Specifically, asynchronous communication is key with timezone differences, and absolutely everything is transparent, so that everyone can stay connected. At the moment we use the following:

Synchronous:

- HipChat: www.worktravel.co/hipchat

- Sqwiggle: www.worktravel.co/sqwiggle

- Mini local meetups

- Retreats (see above)

(See **Chapter 7: Run The Best Biz** for more information on HipChat and Sqwiggle.)

Asynchronous:

- Email

- Hackpad (for collaborating in to-do lists and documents): www.worktravel.co/hackpad

- Discourse (online community software): www.worktravel.co/discourse

- An internal tool we're building

Full disclosure: we also reschedule meetings *constantly*. It's just part of the deal with nomads. It's completely normal to end a meeting with, "So, what timezone will you be in next week?"

- "How we communicate to create customer happiness as a remote team": www.worktravel.co/buffer11

What's it like seeing people in person on the Buffer retreats? Is it weird after you've spent months only ever talking to them on HipChat?!

Haha, no it's surprisingly not weird. Although we do joke that it's fun to see each other's elbows after so many months of video chats!

For photos, search Instagram for #bufferretreat

- "Inside the Buffer retreat": www.worktravel.co/buffer12

Is there anything that the company *can't* do without a physical office? (I.e. is there ever a time when one of you thinks, "Yeah, it'd be kinda useful if we were all in the same place right now"?)

Haha, constantly! Tons of things are easier in-person. Design collaboration is a specific example. Or more broadly, gathering around a table and talking something out is often 10x faster in person. Still, the joys and benefits of being distributed (see www.worktravel.co/buffer2) are totally worth the additional energy. We kind of get the best of both worlds with the freedom to travel and live where we're the happiest, while also making sure that we all work and have dinners and tell stories all together a few times per year.

Crystal Bryant: Developer and writer

Tell us a bit about you and what you do – both in terms of your work and travel habits.

My main income comes from my job as a developer. My main client is my former employer, and I have a contract with them that has me on a "normal" schedule of 40 hours per week (and more when needed). When we left the United States, I also moved from editing as a hobby to editing as a job (see www.crystalraebryant.com). I was very involved with a local writers' group in Nashville for two or three years before we left, and that helped me build both experience and my initial client base. On top of that, I now work on a few side development projects of my own.

Our original intention was to move every three or four months, but we fell in love with a small town and ended up making that our base. I travel back to the US about three times a year for work (face-to-face meetings and conferences) and family. My husband volunteers and I work. I spend my work time on 70% software development, 20% editing, and 10% whatever new idea is on my brain.

What steps did you take to transition towards becoming a digital nomad?

We took a big leap. My husband Jonathan and I had traveled internationally separately before we moved, but only within the US together. He was in state politics, which is very location specific, and I worked full time in an office as a developer.

I had been saying to him for years, even before we got married, that I wanted to live abroad some day. Even if just for a year or so. Once we got married and it became clear how entrenched in his job he was, I began saying that I would do it someday – even if I had to wait until I was 70 and he'd kicked the bucket.

But then the right friend asked the right question at the right time: Why don't you move to Costa Rica, too? And my husband followed that up by asking me, "Can we?"

Ten days (and one very drunken night later), we decided we were going. That was the middle of October 2013. Jonathan left for Costa Rica on Dec 28, 2013 with instructions to find me an apartment with decent internet, and I spent the next three weeks finishing selling, donating, and packing what little we wanted to keep. Then I flew to Costa Rica on January 17, 2014.

We had intended to keep moving every three to four months, but once we landed in Puerto Viejo de Talamanca, Costa Rica, we found a home we hadn't been expecting, and started making this "home base."

What was your main reason for wanting to live this sort of lifestyle?

Freedom. When I was considering what to study in university, I was interested in music, art, writing, and computers. Only one of those (realistically) ended in a non-teaching job, and it also happened to be the one that would most easily let me work from anywhere.

How do you stay productive?

Most of the time, I have a hard time *not* working. Before we left, we had always assumed my husband was the workaholic, working long hours, having a hard time not bringing the job home. Once he had a chance to relax and figure himself out a bit, we realized that *I'm* the true workaholic. Even before we left, I always had a million projects in one stage or another. Now that I am much more relaxed and energized (being in charge of your work environment does that for me), it's very easy for me to focus on projects that can bring in income without feeling overwhelmed or like they're "work."

It helps that at the beginning of my work-from-home stage I had a strict schedule of when people expected me to be online and morning meetings that helped me frame my day. On days where I don't have that schedule, I don't set a specific time for me to start or stop working, but I do set specific tasks that I would like to complete for the day, and fit them in whenever is most convenient.

What's the hardest thing about being a digital nomad?

Learning how to take vacation and learning how to say no. I recently returned from a trip to the US for a conference and had scheduled four days of nothing for when I came back. It was so hard to make myself NOT touch the computer and actually let my brain and body recover.

What tools, equipment or tactics do you rely on for travelling while working?

My iPad is the most important piece of equipment I own while traveling. Second to that is my wireless keyboard and third would be my laptop. When I'm traveling, I often scale back on my development work (it's not necessary, but it helps me balance out the two disparate types of work I do) and I focus on editing and writing. I use Microsoft Office's Word on my iPad to keep track of the changes and notes on documents that I edit.

I pay for a US phone number and unlimited US phone calls

every year, but I rarely use it for business. Almost all of my communication happens on Facebook – something I'm trying to move away from as Facebook is often overwhelming and distracting.

I'm trying to move many of my disparate teams onto Slack (www.worktravel.co/slack) because of this. I already have many of them using Trello (www.worktravel.co/trello), which is easily integrated with Slack.

Mark Gibson: Circus school owner and remote worker

Tell us a bit about you and what you do – both in terms of your work and travel habits.

I have two careers! I work in telecommunications – teaching and managing a globally distributed elearning team. And I have a parallel career in circus: I own and manage a circus school in Glasgow (www.aerialedge.co.uk), where I also teach and perform.

My travel patterns vary wildly. I might be on a teaching tour for telecommunications to any part of the world, or I might be staying in one location creating a circus show or training in something new and interesting. I do travel for the sake of it and make sure I have trips that I take just for the hell of it and work from wherever I am.

I have a base near the circus school in Glasgow, but make sure that I spend time working with other schools around the world – recently in NYC and Brazil. Most of my travel is solo and could be in a hotel, Airbnb (www.worktravel.co/airbnb) or staying with a network of friends. I would normally spend around 50% of my time outside the UK

Did you do the same work before you became a digital nomad?

I did with regards to telecommunications, but I slowly moved from being office-based in London to being remotely based in Scotland, to now being based wherever I like.

The circus school work developed in parallel and was set up to work in a way that ensured that I could still remain nomadic. The school is, however, one of the main reasons to return frequently to Scotland, as there's so much exciting innovative stuff happening there.

What steps did you take to transition towards becoming a digital nomad?

Step by step. It started by taking the opportunity to negotiate a work-from-home contract when a pay rise wasn't possible in my telecommunications job. I then managed to gain a lot of trust when I was working abroad, by showing that I could still get the job done.

What was your main reason for wanting to live this sort of lifestyle?

Firstly to be able to work and travel without sacrificing a lifestyle I enjoy, but mainly now to meet new people and have interesting experiences. Most of the new innovations I've brought into the circus organisation are due to relationships I've built with people I've spent time with while travelling.

Being able to interact with other digitally nomadic entrepreneurs has also enabled me to take a lot of new ideas more frequently seen in start-ups and internet marketing companies back into the world of corporate education.

How do you stay productive?

Easy: I have a great passion for what I do! It's harder to not do it! Having said that, I do have all sorts of productivity systems to ensure I best use the time I have available.

I've also built two great teams who are high performing and love what they do. It's a great collaborative environment.

What does a typical day look like for you?

There are no typical days! Could be building a flying trapeze rig and teaching one day, performing in a show the next or presenting a new education solution to a C-Level executive the day after.

What do you wish you'd known at the start?

That this was both possible and that it would be so much more than just a combination of travel and work!

What's the hardest thing about being a digital nomad?

Perhaps getting people to understand that even if you can't make a face-to-face meeting in their office, work can continue and can be productive! I can't possibly count the times I've had emails that say, "We'll progress this once you are back in January and can talk about it"!

What tools, equipment or tactics do you rely on for travelling while working?

- Zoom (www.worktravel.co/zoom) for video calls with screen sharing.

- Slack (www.worktravel.co/slack) for great team chat and file sharing.

- Omnifocus (www.worktravel.co/omnifocus) for personal task management.

- Asana (www.worktravel.co/asana) for team task management.

- Trello (www.worktravel.co/trello) for project status monitoring.

- Inbox Zero (an approach to email management aimed at

keeping the inbox empty – see www.worktravel.co/inboxzero) for email management.

Lewis Smith: Freelance developer and app creator

Tell us a bit about you and what you do – both in terms of your work and travel habits.

My name is Lewis (aka the Itinerant Dev: www.itinerantdev.com) and I've been travelling with my wife Jenny (www.theadventuresmith.com) since September 2012. I don't feel like "travelling" is the right word anymore. Really we live in a place for a few months and then move on. For example, we're in Mexico at the moment and we'll be here for five months in total and we'll stay in three places. We don't really have a base and if we go "home" [the UK] we stay with friends or our parents. I think the optimal amount of time is about three months in one place.

I work as a web and mobile developer (I built Find A Nomad, for example: www.worktravel.co/findanomad), and I switch between freelancing and making my own apps. All of the freelance work I do is either for companies I worked for in the UK before I left or from recommendations. (I've actually met two of my clients either directly or indirectly through The Anywhereist Group – www.worktravel.co/anywhereist – which is an online community for digital nomads.)

What did you do before you became a digital nomad?

Programming is my profession, but I had only done a little freelancing.

What steps did you take to transition towards becoming a digital nomad? (Or did it just happen naturally?)

The main thing we did was save a load of money so we had a buffer if things went wrong. I also took on a freelance gig from peopleperhour.com but luckily I haven't needed to rely on work like that since. We actually transitioned within about six months. It's amazing how much money you can save when you put your mind to it.

If you are planning to freelance I'd recommend trying to get some work before you set off – either by networking or using one of the freelance sites. Once you have one or two clients who you do a great job for, they won't mind you working overseas. This probably means working evenings or weekends initially, but it will be worth it, plus you get some extra buffer funds. Don't be afraid to ask your current employer for work too. Finding new staff is tough and if you were doing a good job they'll likely be really happy to come to an arrangement with you, even if it's just a transition period.

What was your main reason for wanting to live this sort of lifestyle?

We had lived in the same town all our lives. After going on honeymoon to Thailand we realised there was so much more to the world and we wanted to go see it. Our initial plan was to backpack around the world, but as time went on we realised we didn't want or need to go home to live or work.

How do you stay productive?

I'm a bit of a productivity geek and I love my work so I don't find it a big struggle. Plus I only get paid for work I do so that keeps me motivated!

The biggest thing you can do for this is to not move around too much and to either find a nice apartment or even better a nice co-working space to work from. Most friction comes from lack of knowledge about a place and losing time to learning. The less you move the more local knowledge you have.

What does a typical day look like for you?

In a lot of ways it's not that different from most people:

- Get up

- Do a little meditation (Maybe that's different? But not specific to being overseas)

- Go to a coworking space and work

- Go someplace nice for lunch

- Do more work

- Go for a jog or a walk (jogging is one of my favourite ways to see a new place)

- Have dinner someplace nice

- Drink some wine and watch some TV, or meet up with new friends

- Go to bed

Going someplace nice to eat is easier when you are not at home, especially if you are in a cheaper country.

On weekends or days off we try and do a tour or go visit a museum – you know, the tourist stuff. You have an instant vacation then, which is really nice.

What do you wish you'd known at the start?

The slower you go the less stressful it is. You'll make more friends, get to know a place better and feel like you really fit in. You'll be more productive too and enjoy your time off more.

Also, don't worry too much about "stuff". Having a nice backpack or amazing travel clothes is great and all, but really it's trivial compared to having money in the bank and a positive outlook. You can buy anything you need in most places.

What's the hardest thing about being a digital nomad?

Getting set up with basics when you first move to a new place is the hardest thing now. It's easy to find the best restaurant on review sites, but finding a nice cheap place for breakfast or lunch everyday takes a little while to find. Good places to work can be tough to find too. I tend to just default to coworking spaces these days.

Making new friends can be tricky in a new place too. The best thing for this is also to head to a co-working space, but we've also used meetup.com a few times and couch surfer meetups can be good too. And, of course, Find A Nomad (www.worktravel.co/findanomad) is a great way to plan a trip where you know you'll meet great people.

What tools, equipment or tactics do you rely on for working while travelling?

Hardware wise, nothing different from at home. I have a bunch of things for my RSI – a laptop riser and separate keyboard and mouse. Good headphones are vital for me too – I use SoundMagic E10 Earphones (www.worktravel.co/soundmagic).

I also live out of my iPhone and use Google Maps and Foursquare a lot. Foursquare (www.worktravel.co/foursquare) is better than TripAdvisor and Yelp for getting local recommendations in my experience. Google Translate (www.worktravel.co/gtranslate) is fantastic these days too, I'm still amazed that you can point your phone at the side of a box or a sign and Google can translate the text for you in real time. [See **Chapter 1: Settle In Fast** for more ideas on how to use Google Translate.]

There's a Mac App called World Clock (www.worktravel.co/worldclock), which is useful for checking the times back home (or around the world) for meetings etc. Shameless plug: my app World Time Widget (www.worktravel.co/timewidget) does the same thing on iPhone.

Having a local SIM makes life so much easier. [See **Chapter 1: Settle In Fast** for more information about buying a local SIM.]

Airbnb (www.worktravel.co/airbnb) can be good for finding accommodation.

Blake Boles: Adventure company owner

Can you provide a bit of information about what you do and how you got into it?

My company, Unschool Adventures (www.unschooladventures.com), leads international trips and U.S.-based educational programs for self-directed young adults.

In a nutshell, I lead groups of ~10 teenagers (ages 14-19) on 4- to 6-week-long international trips that are focused on exploration, cultural immersion, and learning to become an independent traveler (recent destinations include Argentina, New Zealand and Nepal). I also lead 4- to 10-week-long domestic programs [i.e. in America] that focus more on creativity and leadership skills (recent programs include the Writing Retreat and this year's Adventure Semester).

Every program is different (with the exception of the Writing Retreat, which we've done 4 times) and you can get a pretty good feeling for what they're like by skimming each program's webpage: www.unschooladventures.com/previous-trips

Most of the kids who sign up for these trips are self-described "unschoolers". In the beginning I recruited most of them from Not Back to School Camp, a summer camp where I've worked since 2006, but quickly word-of-mouth and my presentations at conferences took over, to the point where now I don't know most of the kids signing up.

Trips cost between $1,800 (4-week Writing Retreat) and $5,000 (6-week New Zealand trip) and I don't offer scholarships. Most of the kids are from middle- and middle-upper class families who are already doing something "alternative" with their kids' educations.

Running these programs has provided the lion's share of my income for the past ~6 years. My books (or at least the two self-published ones) also bring in a little side income.

These books focus on issues related to designing your own education and thinking hard about the college/university decision. I mostly write for a teenage/college-aged audience (even if it's more the parents who pick up the book first). Find out more about the books here: www.blakeboles.com/my-books.

The books and trips reinforce each other nicely! I crowdfunded the publishing costs ($6,000-$9,000) of both of my self-published books as well as a few other projects.

What steps did you take to create your business and get it up and running?

Funny story.

I decided to start Unschool Adventures after interviewing to work as an trip leader for, and ultimately getting rejected by, an established gap year travel company. A few days later I emailed the director (same guy who interviewed me) and said "Hey, I still really want to do this work, so could you help me start my own company so I can take these teen unschoolers around the world?" He graciously said yes and then shared a bunch of his company's paperwork and policies with me. He also connected me to his group travel specialist who I continue to use to this day.

With all that, all I did next was file the LLC paperwork, whip together a website (I knew enough HTML/CSS/Photoshop to do it myself) and asked the director of Not Back to School Camp to share the website with the camp community via email.

How does your business find new "clients" (i.e. people to participate in the Unschool Adventures retreats and programs)?

I do virtually zero paid advertising: maybe a promoted FB post every blue moon. It all happens through word of mouth through the home/unschooling conference and camp world. I notice a big boost in applications when I'm giving talks/workshops at conferences. All my books also mention Unschool Adventures.

How do you find staff? How do you train and manage them?

Every international program has 2-3 staff (at least one of each sex) and domestic programs have 4+. I mostly recruit current/former staff from the Not Back to School Camp and Deer Crossing Camp (a wilderness summer camp in CA where I worked / assistant directed for a long time) worlds.

Summer camp staffers just "get" the whole mentality better than anyone else. Mostly they're my friends. I do little training. I do look for staff with high levels of safety credentials (Wilderness First Responder / EMT). On our programs we're like a big family; "management" is a funny word that doesn't seem to apply.

I should mention that I'm always a primary trip leader on our international trips. I've tried to offer international trips with other leaders (not myself) but they've never filled (and therefore were cancelled). I think I've built myself into the Unschool Adventures brand too much – it's kind of a problem.

I've had more success having other people run the Writing Retreat program. In the future I'm going to continue getting former Unschool Adventures staff to try creating and running domestic programs on their own. In those cases I typically want to see a long work history of managing/designing long-term immersive teen programs before I'd consider letting that person take the reigns without me. I guess I'm pretty protective of my programs and brand name :)

What are your travel habits like? What dictates where you'll go and how long you'll be there?

I pretty much design our international trips around whichever country I've personally been hankering to visit for a while... ha! (That's definitely how the company started. I had recently spent 3 months in South America and desperately wanted to return to Argentina. So I designed the first Unschool Adventures trip in 2008 to be 6 weeks in Argentina.)

Where we'll go is determined by a balance of culture, outdoors, safety, and price. You can't have them all, of course. Argentina I think still has a great balance of all those (I've taken 4 groups there). Another important factor is hard to describe... I call it the "low-expectation" factor. Essentially if you're going to France and you want to do something off the beaten path, everyone and their mother will say "Oh you're going to France and *not* doing the Louvre? *How could you?*" as if I'm an axe murderer. France and the rest of Western Europe carries all these expectations about things you *must do* otherwise your trip is a waste. But a place like Argentina or New Zealand comes with fewer expectations. So the teens are more open to doing something a little different, weird, and (I believe) ultimately more fun and interesting.

How long we'll go is dictated by:

1) Getting the most out of an expensive international plane

ticket – I consider 4 weeks to be the absolute minimum for an international trip; 6 much better.

2) Not making the trip so long that the price gets inflated. Although my trips cost a pretty penny they're still *way* cheaper than most other organized group programs, which is a point of pride.

3) Keeping the length appropriate for a teen who's never been out of the country before and has maybe only spent 1-2 weeks away from home ever before in life.

For the domestic trips, I still try to aim for 4 weeks or more, because big life changes take more than a week. And there's a lot of competition for those short time periods… not so much in the 4-10 week range.

Oh and I almost never run programs in the summertime (June-August) because there's tons of competition from traditional summer programs and I personally like to have my summer free to enjoy the outdoors. That's the great thing about serving the home/unschooler community: you can take trips in any time of the year! We have enjoyed lots of off-season travel benefits.

What is it about this lifestyle that you're attracted to?

1) Getting paid to design trips that I think are fun+meaningful and then personally lead them with groups of really nice/smart/creative teens who I genuinely like being around.

2) The seasonality of the work: make a lot of money in a short

period of time, and then enjoy big blocks of mostly free time.

3) Seeing more of the world, of course!

4) Feeling like I'm making a big difference in the lives of a handful of young people.

What do you wish you'd known when you started?

I could have probably charged more money than I thought :)

What tools, equipment or tactics do you rely on for working while travelling?

- MailboxForwarding (www.worktravel.co/mailbox) – a godsend for not missing important mail. I got it after struggling to deal with an IRS inquiry that arrived via snail mail in 2011 when I was leading a 7-week trip in Argentina, Chile, and Peru. Now all my mail gets scanned and emailed to me upon arrival.

    [See **Chapter 1: Settle In Fast** for more information on mail-forwarding services.]

- Sucuri (www.worktravel.co/sucuri) – protecting my websites from stupid hackers/malware. This came out of a terrible experience in 2013 when all my websites went down when my New Zealand group was volunteering at a picturesque farm. I was inside using the owner's computer for a few days trying to get everything back online. Now I just pay some really smart guys to monitor and fix that stuff for me.

- When Lonely Planet started selling individual PDF chapters (www.worktravel.co/chapters), I was psyched. [They're also available as MOBI and ePub files.]

- HelpX (www.worktravel.co/helpx) for finding informal and zero-cost (but still vetted) group-volunteering opportunities.

- My Patagonia MLC bag (www.worktravel.co/mlc).

Kathryn O'Halloran: Romance fiction writer

Tell us a bit about you and what you do – both in terms of your work and travel habits.

I'm a writer. My main source of income is from writing romance under a pen name. I self publish and have my novels for sale on Amazon, Apple, B&N and most other major retailers. I publish directly on Amazon and, for the rest, use a distributor called Draft 2 Digital (www.worktravel.co/draft). They take a cut of my royalties but make the process a whole lot easier. Also, they pay into my PayPal account which is so much better than dealing with bank transfers or even cheques!

I also write under my real name (www.kathrynohalloran.com/books). I must be the only writer who publishes erotica under my real name and has a pen name for the other stuff (like the romance novels), but I started submitting erotic shorts to anthologies years ago and never thought to use a pen name. The stuff I write under my real name is more literary and not nearly as marketable though. It's more like hobby writing than something I do for profit.

In order to be financially viable, I have an intense publishing schedule. I released a three-book series this year and plan to release another three novels before the end of the year. That whole image of the tortured writer, sitting around for years waiting for their muse to visit… forget about it. Romance is a competitive market and if I don't have new work coming out, I don't make money.

I'd thought about self publishing for a while and decided to go for it at the end of 2012.

For about a year, I toyed around and made a little money. There are certain strategies that tend to be successful in self-publishing but I thought I was a special snowflake who didn't need that kind of thing. Then, one day, I woke up (literally) with this plan to write a three-book romance series using those strategies to see if they worked, writing purely to a specific market.

That ended up working better than I expected. My writing

income jumped from double figures per month to triple then quadruple. For one heady month, I hit five figures. Without promotion, I now get a fairly consistent four-figure income a month. I'm lucky because I've kind of developed a bit of a niche for my writing. Well, partly lucky and partly it's come about from studying the market and working out what sells.

Some people have issues with writing to market and the whole "doing it for money not love" thing, but to me it's like a venn diagram – you find the intersection between what you love writing and what people want to buy and work within that space.

Writing is, in some ways, the perfect profession if you want to travel. It's pretty much always been a job you do remotely back when you had to handwrite your manuscript and mail it off to publishers. Thank goodness those days are long behind us. With the emergence of self-publishing the barriers to becoming a writer have pretty much disappeared but, to make a living, there is a lot more work thrown back on the writer. You don't have a publisher or agent to handle the business side of things (or take you to boozy lunches, unfortunately).

Sometimes I feel like my home base is my laptop. It's the only thing I need for work and pretty much my life. I do have a storage space though. Because I'd been sharing a place with my sister, we had a lot of joint-owned stuff that I need to keep. Otherwise, a storage space is probably the worst option. It's a nightmare to access and not cheap. I'd have preferred to just get rid of most of my stuff.

My travel plans at the moment are based around being in certain places at certain times I'm house-sitting for a friend in Geneva in August and wanted to be in Japan for my birthday in September. Then I'll be in Tokyo at the end of the year because my favourite J-pop band is touring then. In between, I look for places that are cheap and interesting and fit in with my other plans.

I travel on my own but also try to work in some time with friends in various countries.

I've been moving around a fair bit lately – some of that unplanned as I've had a bit of bad luck with Airbnb hosts.

Ideally, I think a month is the absolute minimum time to spend in a place unless you want to treat it more like a vacation rather than work time just because of the overheads of learning your way around a new city, finding cafes and all that.

I'm still working on finding the best way to do things and what my priorities are. Access to coffee is always high on the list and ergonomic working conditions are important.

What did you do before you became a digital nomad? (Were you still a romance writer, or did you do a different job entirely?)

I worked in IT for years as a programmer and data analyst. It seems like a huge jump but even working in IT, I was happiest working on contracts where I could manage my own projects from the beginning stages all the way through to rollout – which is a very similar way of working to what I do with my writing.

A big issue for me was that I felt like the skills I had in IT were eroding and I either needed to make an investment getting back to a level where I could be competitive in the marketplace or try something else. I went for the something else.

What steps did you take to transition towards becoming a digital nomad? (Or did it just happen naturally?)

I didn't really take so many conscious steps. It has been a slow untethering. I quit working in a permanent job over ten years ago and became a contractor when I realised that contracting meant more money and also the ability to totally sidestep things like team development meetings and office politics. Funny how those things become a lot less important when you are being paid by the hour.

I loved the flexibility of contracting. Even though I worked on site for clients, I could plan travel around different projects. I'd start a contract and have people tell me that maybe, if I was lucky, I'd get a permanent job out of it, but that freaked me out. I hated the idea of having someone else decide when I could take holidays or even my working hours.

Then, about two years ago, I was coming to the end of a year-long contract and my writing income had grown from just coffee money (although for me, coffee money is quite substantial). I had a decent amount of cash in the bank so figured I'd focus on writing for a while. If an opportunity had presented itself to go back to IT contracting, I'd have probably taken it but I wasn't actively looking for that next contract.

I have very low living costs anyway. I got rid of my car a few years ago, I have no dependents and no debt. My only real indulgence is travel so it wasn't long before I could exist just on my writing income.

I spent part of last year travelling but more as a break between writing books rather than working on the road (i.e. I left the laptop at home but still did a lot of marketing and admin work). I guess it was more like an intermittent travel/work thing – working flat out to get work released, then taking time off to travel.

I shared a place with my sister for quite a few years and she'd get housemates in while I was travelling. It worked out quite well because I had all my stuff there and a place to come home to without any expenses.

The impetus to make travel a more permanent arrangement came from reading blogs by digital nomads and realising that it really was an affordable option. The cost of living in Australia is pretty high and rent is insane. I became addicted to reading other people's budget posts. It's a total epiphany to know that you don't need to be earning huge money or have massive savings in order to live a nomadic lifestyle and it can be much cheaper than staying put.

Around the same time, our living situation was becoming impossible. Half the people in our street were renovating and the noise levels were insane. Not even noise-cancelling headphones helped. It drives me insane that people can get all these workmen in during the day and go off to work away from the noise while those of us who work from home have to deal with it.

So my sister and I decided to move back in with our mum for a while. If I could time-travel, I'd bitch-slap myself for thinking that was a good decision! It did make me very motivated to get overseas though.

What was your main reason for wanting to live this sort of lifestyle?

Why wouldn't I? It's the perfect life :) The fact that I can write novels and travel around the world at the same time is a dream come true.

I love being completely self-indulgent and following my own schedule. For many years, I wanted to travel and get out of the corporate world but I was a single mum and had commitments plus always seemed to struggle financially. Then my son left home and I could suddenly do what I want and had so much more money. Now if I run out of money, I can call him to bail me out.

How do you stay productive?

This is a big issue for me because I am the queen of procrastination. I need to get myself into panic mode so that I actually do stuff.

Of course, money is big motivator. No work, no money coming

in. But also I find if I make a financial commitment, I can't back down from that. I don't have anyone else giving me deadlines so I build them in and put money behind them – booking editors, paying for release promotions that kind of thing. When I've made that commitment, I'm too much of a cheapskate to risk losing my money.

After I've done that, I work backwards so that I have a daily word count to meet. I use rewards, usually sleep rewards like if I write another thousand words I can have a nap. I also have everything detailed in my spreadsheet and try to beat my last highest word count.

One of the things I am constantly working on to increase my productivity is writing clean drafts – using outlining techniques so that I have the novel structure in place before I start writing ends up being a huge time saver in the overall span of a project (I guess that is also like IT work: getting the "specifications" in place before starting work).

I don't have any techniques I use. I've tried things like Pomodoro (www.worktravel.co/pomodoro) but I don't like that kind of structure. The main thing for me is getting started because it's a lot like travel: I have to leave the "real world" and get immersed in this other place.

I've been thinking of getting a virtual assistant (VA) for a while now so that I don't have to focus so much on admin stuff. I kept a spreadsheet for a month, breaking down what I did into writing, administration and non-work by the hour, and was really surprised at how much time went into the administration side. And, even with spending that amount of time, there is a lot that I let slide because it's not directly related to my income. I do very little social media, for example.

The problem with getting a VA is that I either need to research to find someone who is experienced with this field or invest time in training someone, so it keeps getting pushed to the bottom of the pile. I do outsource a bit, using people who set up blog tours or act as intermediaries with reviewers and, of course, editing and cover design is outsourced.

What does a typical day look like for you?

I have the worst schedule. It's something I really need to work on.

I wake up early, usually about 6am but I hate waking up early so pretty much every day I think I'll go back to sleep but never do.

If I'm awake, I need coffee. If I want to get some sightseeing done, I'll get out and about before breakfast because I hate crowds. I'd much rather go for a walk around in the early morning before most tourists have gotten out of bed.

Otherwise I'll muck around on the internet. That includes checking sales figures, reading forums, doing admin stuff like booking advertising and answering fan emails. Plus working out travel arrangements and all that kind of thing. Usually I think about writing but put it off.

Often I'll nap after lunch. I love napping a lot.

Then I have a mad panic that I've not got any work done so get stuck into the actual writing. Once I get started, I am pretty efficient.

I'll often stay up half the night working. One of my mental tricks is to get a good word count on my spreadsheet for the day so I get up the next day with lots of words already written. That spurs me on to write even more.

It seems that no matter what time I go to bed though, I'm always awake super early.

What's the hardest thing about being a digital nomad?

The hardest thing, I find is finding balance. Travel is all about being in the moment while writing is about being off somewhere in your head. It can be hard to switch between the two. The "being in the moment" thing is so important too. It's not just about appreciating that sunset that you'll never see again (although that is important or why travel in the first place?), but knowing where all your belongings are and if that weird man is actually following you or just walking down the same street. Those kinds of practical concerns where you need to have your head out of the clouds.

Actually, the really hardest thing is that I miss my dog (she's actually my sister's dog and I get yelled at for calling her mine). With humans, they can understand why you are leaving and know you'll be back. With technology nowadays, it's so easy to keep in touch. But dogs don't understand. You can't even Skype because it's confusing for them to hear your voice and not be able to see or smell you.

What tools, equipment or tactics do you rely on for working while travelling?

My laptop is, of course, my most important bit of equipment. I use a Windows laptop – I stopped using Apple products after the time my iPod broke the day after the warranty expired – although there are some advantages to Macs. At the moment, I have my books on iBooks through a distributor. To list and sell books directly, you do need to have a Mac, of course. When I replace this laptop though, I'm thinking about getting a Chromebook.

For writing, I use Scrivener (www.worktravel.co/scrivener – writing software). I've not been too happy with it lately though and have lost work a couple of times so am looking around for an alternative. For shorter works, I just use MS Word. I also use Word for editing because of the "track changes" feature.

One of the handiest features of Word, that I've only learnt about six months ago, is the text-to-speech function. It's about as much fun as root canals, but listening through my drafts catches a crap ton of errors before I send stuff off to the editor.

I include Calibre (www.worktravel.co/calibre) for converting files to different formats and both Canva (www.worktravel.co/canva) and Picmonkey (www.worktravel.co/picmonkey) to make graphics for promo stuff.

That's pretty much it for the writing side. Of course, having a decent wifi connection is important but less so than most remote work. I'm not transferring large files or uploading that often. I would like to get some kind of wifi booster though. I just need to do more research into them.

For admin, everything is in MS Excel. All my sales numbers and projections, expenses, the works. A lot of writers I talk to are vague about the whole business side of thing but I have all the data. If someone asked me how many books I sold in Germany in March 2012, I'd be able to tell them within seconds – as well as how it compared to my average sales and the sales for the previous year.

For goal-setting, I use a lot of conditional formatting so things go a pretty colour when I'm on top of them. It's probably overkill but I worked in data analysis and I love having all that information at my fingertips.

The most important data for me, apart from knowing where my money is coming from and how much I'm going to get is being able to set benchmarks. If I start writing a series and it doesn't meet the benchmarks I expect then I scrap further projects – that kind of thing.

I've gotten used to working on screen which is really handy because it'd be a total pain having to deal with printing out drafts while travelling.

Which countries/cities would you recommend for people who are new to travelling while they work?

That's a really difficult question and so dependent on your priorities and needs. I hate sun and beaches so I tend to shy away from places that a lot of digital nomads like.

Something I've been thinking about a lot is project-based travel, for want of a better term. A few years ago, I was doing research for an historical novel I was working on (and have never finished – historicals are so hard). I travelled a lot in Japan with a really sharp focus on research I needed for my writing. I think that can be a lot more interesting to travel when you have an actual project or learning experience you want to achieve rather than just a random "must see" list.

So, rather than suggesting a specific travel destination, I'd suggest looking at places that tie in with the work you do or hobbies/interests – whether that's foodie stuff, martial arts, Renaissance art, rare breeds of spiders or whatever. After spending a bit of time in a location, that becomes more satisfying than just "oh look, pretty castle…"

How do you make new friends/keep in touch with old ones while travelling?

I'm not really a "making friends" kind of person. I get a bit annoyed when I read blog posts and things about travel for introverts because the blogger is all about getting out of your comfort zone and making friends, not really understanding the difference between being an introvert and being shy. It's something I try to cover a bit on my blog because introverts need to be given ways to cope with situations rather than have the implication that something that is basically at the core of their personality needs changing.

I actually find it strange that one of the first things solo travellers want to do is meet other people, like they'd rather do something with a complete stranger who might be a boring twat than be alone.

The only time I've regretted travelling alone is in Seoul because most of the BBQ places have a two-person minimum. I had my nose pressed to the glass like the Little Matchgirl craving that delicious meat. Oh, and the other day at Bratislava train station when I discovered the toilets were down a very steep flight of stairs to the basement. I had a dodgy back already and looked at my luggage then at those stairs and decided to hold on until I was on the train. In those kinds of situations, I'd like to make friends quick smart.

When I do meet up with people, it's usually because I know them online either through my blog or other sites. Then it's more a case of wanting to meet someone because I find them interesting and want to get to know them rather than just hanging out with the nearest available person to avoid being alone.

I spend a lot of time keeping in touch with family. At the moment, my mother has been ill and in and out of hospital so I've tried to stay as available as I can. Mostly through Facebook. My mum and sister live in rural Tasmania where the internet is far too shonky to make Skype an option. I was actually going to delete my Facebook account recently because I have issues with their ethics but so many of my friends complained that I kept it going.

This is going to make me sound like a total weirdo but, because I miss my sister's dog so much, I said I'd send her postcards. But, being a dog, she can't read so I send her smells. Usually delicious food smells. None of the postcards have reached her yet though so I wonder if the mail-checking postal dogs have devoured them.

Pete Domican: Remote management consultant

Tell us a bit about you and what you do – both in terms of your work and travel habits.

Professionally, I'm a management consultant (www.onetreeless.com) specialising in strategy and transformation – i.e. helping companies decide what to do and then do it. I've worked for major consultancies, independently and as a contractor or as part of a group of fellow independents. Over my career I've worked with both large corporates such as Airbus and Sky and small clients with around 50 employees. I'm also involved in a new business startup and I'm a committee member of the Levitt Group, which is the special interest group for Chartered and Fellow marketers in the Chartered Institute of Marketing.

I'm also a photographer (www.peterdomican.zenfolio.com) and writer – although they don't provide any significant income. I'm a Licentiate of the Royal Photographic Society and much of my desire to travel comes from the photographic opportunities new places present.

I consider myself a "semi digital nomad". I'm digital but not really a full nomad in the sense of "roaming around". I have a house just outside London but I can work from anywhere, as long as I don't need to be on a client site. If I do, I try to find clients in more interesting places and combine work and travel. I'm single so I don't need to go home every weekend – e.g. I recently did some work with an Icelandic company, which enabled me to spend time in Reykjavik. I also have a slight (major) obsession with Lisbon so I want to spend more time out there in the future.

The important thing for me is to be able to take advantage of any opportunity without having to think too much about location as a barrier. Recently I spent a day with Olympus Cameras photographing a circus but if I'd have had an urgent client request, I could have got out my Mac, sent a file, amended a presentation, etc. without it ruining the entire day.

Did you do the same work before you became a digital nomad? Are there any limits to you being able to work as a

full digital nomad?

I've been working in management consultancy or change/project management since my MBA, so the work is pretty much the same. It's important for me to spend time with clients in order to understand their environment, issues and culture but equally being on site all the time can be counterproductive.

The chances of me winning and completing a contract from a hammock in Chang Mai are pretty much zero but, with agile tools like JIRA and modern communications, more of the work can be done away from the client site. The major limiting factor now is not so much the technology but how willing clients are to embrace it.

What steps did you take to transition towards becoming a digital nomad? (Or did it just happen naturally?)

It's been a naturally evolving process. I first thought about the idea of working remotely about ten years ago when I was spending a lot of time out in Canada skiing. You could "work" remotely with the existing technology (in a fashion) but you were still highly constrained by speed and reliability – e.g. 56k modems. It was flaky and unprofessional.

Big consultancy companies eventually made remote working possible but then made life difficult again by having laptops with Windows Vista – so I often spent a large chunk of my day on the phone to a help desk and not doing my job.

Now with a Mac and Wifi or 4G Mifi, I can work almost

anywhere and it's pretty seamless. I've worked on presentations in a coastal fort in Portugal and sent emails from the backseat of a car travelling through the French Alps.

What was your main reason for wanting to live this sort of lifestyle?

In the space of about nine months, I had a relationship breakup and also left my job at a major firm. The role wasn't what I'd hoped it would be when I joined and I'd stayed in the role longer than I should have done for the sake of my relationship. I'd put a lot of effort into trying to please everyone and it hadn't worked out, so it was a difficult period trying to come to terms with things and figure out what to do going forward.

I decided that I wanted to go back to what I'd been doing in previous roles but that I really needed to get a better kind of balance between work and creative projects.

I wanted to travel more and do work that I believed in rather than doing things that were "good for my career" (which often seemed to be the stuff other people didn't seem to want to do either). If you're single and going to spend 12 hours a day working, you need to enjoy what you do.

I also spent a lot of time looking at how cloud computing and apps like Dropbox were breaking the stranglehold of IT departments ("Server Huggers" as one of my friends calls them). Being able to work remotely just seemed to be an evolving solution to what I wanted to do.

How do you stay productive?

Staying productive is a challenge. I'm very good with client deadlines. I try to set myself artificial deadlines for admin tasks and non-client projects just to stop me drifting. There's a bit of a conflict with my creative side where there is little correlation between time and quality/quantity of output, and doing "nothing" can be part of the process.

What does a typical day look like for you?

There's no such thing as a typical day for me and that's both a blessing and a curse.

On full-time client work, it's pretty much a conventional office existence but a 12-hour day would be pretty normal whether I'm on the client site or not.

When working on my own things, I tend to get up later (I am not an early bird), do low-level admin work first then get into gear with things that require creativity or critical thinking later in the day. If I'm doing photography/travelling, I'll work around the weather and the light. In the middle of the Icelandic winter, there's about two to three hours of good daylight, so that's pretty easy!

How do you find new clients?

Most clients come through my network: either people I've worked with in the past or I know through my MBA. I also work with other independent consultants/small firms where there's a need for a small team rather than an individual person.

Clients get a much more highly experienced team than they would if they used a large consultancy and at a much cheaper rate.

Over the last couple of years, I've started to become more involved with technology projects so I'm looking to develop opportunities in London's Tech City, which is half an hour away from home.

What's the hardest thing about this lifestyle?

I've just turned 50 and a lot of my friends see this "lifestyle" as a form of extended mid-life crisis. It's hard to talk about what I'm doing with people of my own age. I'm excited by technology but many people seem to regard it with great scepticism based on a lifetime of software not really working properly and under-delivering. It's difficult to explain what you're doing sometimes or get some sensible life advice from people who've known you the longest.

The flipside is you get to meet people who do get it. One of my business colleagues is in a different country every week and there are some really welcoming communities of people who just seem to embrace diversity – like fellow members of The Anywhereist Group (www.worktravel.co/anywhereist).

Eli Trier: Artist, author and illustrator

Tell us a bit about you and what you do – both in terms of your work and travel habits.

I'm an artist, author and illustrator (www.elitrier.com). My primary work is illustration and I also write and illustrate non-fiction picture books for adults. Travel-wise, I'm at the beginning of my nomadic journey – I've been in Copenhagen, Denmark for a couple of months and I'm off to Spain in the autumn. After that, stints in Germany, the US, South America – I'm on a mission to soak up as much of the world as I can.

I travel solo, I'm a single lady with no kids so that's easy, and I like not to have too many plans in advance. I like to go wherever the wind blows me: sometimes I'll go somewhere for work, or to spend time with friends, or just because I like the idea of a place.

What did you do before you became a digital nomad? (Did

you do the same sort of work, or something entirely different?)

I used to work in marketing with a proper day job, then I became a freelance marketing communications consultant but I just wasn't satisfied, or happy. So I followed my heart and it took me out of my career, out of my relationship, and out of the country! I've never been happier.

What steps did you take to transition towards becoming a digital nomad? (Or did it just happen naturally?)

I tend to jump in with both feet, so that's exactly what I did. Travelling is something I've wanted to do my whole life and the time was just right to go for it.

What was your main reason for wanting to live this sort of lifestyle?

Freedom. And movement. I'm happiest when I'm in motion and not tied down to any one thing. This lifestyle suits me very well.

How do you stay productive?

I love my work – I set loose deadlines and work when I feel like it. Luckily I feel like it a lot of the time.

How do you find new clients?

Online, and through word of mouth.

What do you wish you'd known at the start?

How much fun it was and how easy. I could have done this years ago, and I should have.

What's the hardest thing about being a digital nomad?

I miss my friends and family back in England. But that's all, really.

How do you make new friends/keep in touch with old ones while travelling?

The internet! We're so lucky we live in the digital age. One of my best friends in Copenhagen came from a comment she made on a blog we both follow on Facebook. She happened to mention she lived in Copenhagen so I sent her a friend request. She turned out to be an amazing human being and I am blessed that we're now firm friends.

I do love Tinder for exploring a new city as well. A little unconventional, perhaps, but I've met some amazing people who have introduced me to their friends and I've built some really close connections. Be careful, though: there are some weirdos out there (that goes for men and women!).

As for old friends, a combination of Viber, Whatsapp, Skype, Facebook and email ensures I can stay connected with everyone. I'm diligent about maintaining my friendships. My people are the most important thing in my life.

Jewels Velky: Photographer and consultant

Tell us a bit about you and what you do – both in terms of your work and travel habits.

I'm a photographer and consultant in the technology and entrepreneurship space (www.julievelky.com).

I mainly travel with my husband Zach, and then I also have the occasional solo trip.

We're slow travelers and prefer to have at least four weeks in one place so that we can live like the locals, enjoy the sights, and get work done. We have two sweet dogs who we miss while travelling so we're currently setting up our home base back in Austin, TX and plan to focus on North American destinations the next few years with six-week overseas trips every so often.

I love challenging, new things so I typically have one main gig going and then a few side projects. One of the side projects inevitably flourishes and ends up becoming my main gig and that runs on about a two-year cycle, which always keeps me engaged and learning new things.

What did you do before you became a digital nomad? (Did you do the same sort of work, or something entirely different?)

I was working as a writer for an MBA program in entrepreneurship and ended up managing the technical development team that built out an online delivery platform for the MBA school. On the side, I started a contemporary portrait studio which took off and soon required more time, so I re-negotiated my agreement with the business school so I could balance having one foot in photography and one still in the tech/business world.

What steps did you take to transition towards becoming a digital nomad? (Or did it just happen naturally?)

I grew up in a fairly nomadic family who moved back and forth between Canada and Texas multiple times throughout my childhood, so I crave a continual change of scenery. I'd been living in Austin for a few years and was feeling stagnant when a few events stacked up and all signs pointed at getting the hell out and dodge for a while. First, I was bit by a copperhead snake – I survived (obv.) but did have to take some time off from shooting in my portrait studio. Then the house that my husband and I had been renting for the past three years was sold and we were given 30 days' notice. I was upset for about an hour and then my imagination kicked in and I started seeing all of this as THE BEST THING TO EVER HAPPEN. Within weeks I'd put our motorcycles in storage, got rid of just about everything else, shifted my tech work from employee to location-independent contractor, took an official sabbatical from portraiture, and booked a pair of one-way tickets overseas.

What was your main reason for wanting to live this sort of lifestyle?

Agency. I want to have control over what I'm doing, where I am, and who I'm spending my time with. I love working but I hate the bullshit constraints that typically come with "jobs" and have nothing to do with getting your work done effectively.

How do you stay productive?

I have no problem getting work done but I do have a problem letting work creep into all hours of my day, which isn't productive either.

I periodically reassess my schedule and build in mandated "work-free" time – this forces me to be much more efficient when I am working and lets me filter which of my tasks are actually critical paths and which are simply time-wasters and should be shelved.

How do you find new clients?

Almost always by personal referral or former colleagues reaching out to me.

What do you wish you'd known at the start?

Just how much I was going to love Thailand – I would have got to SE Asia sooner and stayed longer. This is top of my return list.

What's the hardest thing about being a digital nomad?

1: We actually have two of the sweetest little fur-children (a black pug and a frenchbo), and I hate leaving them behind even though their grandparents fight over them. SO we've bought a house to home-base out of in Austin, TX and try to limit each of our overseas trips to about six weeks at a time and spend the rest of the time travelling places we can take the dogs with us.

2: Having a different travel style than your spouse/travel buddy! I err on the side of intense drill-sargeant, be-early-or-the-world-might-end on travel days and my husband is the opposite, totally go with the flow, not a worry in the world. So it took some practice for us to get into a rhythm that made travel days work well for both of us and didn't end in a relationship melt-down at an airport check-in counter.

What tools, equipment or tactics do you rely on for working

while travelling?

- Macbook Air

- Samsung Galaxy Note 4 + folding bluetooth keyboard (www.worktravel.co/foldingkeyboard)

- Sony a5000 digital camera (www.worktravel.co/sony) + lenses + Pedco UltraPod II camera tripod (www.worktravel.co/tripod)

- Osprey Farpoint 55L Pack (www.worktravel.co/osprey) – the zip-off daypack is perfect for throwing my electronics in and heading out for the day

- Housesitting – "rent free" peace and quiet with a decent internet connection

Adam and Lindsey Nubern: Accountant and social media consultant

Tell us a bit about you and what you do – both in terms of your work and travel habits.

I (Adam) am a Certified Public Accountant (www.nuventurecpa.com). Lindsey works with various startups on their marketing. We both write the occasional article for online publications.

We have been traveling for 13 months now. It has been an evolution to say the least. We started on a four-month road trip of the US. Then we spent one month on Kauai, five months campervanning New Zealand, and then some time backpacking SE Asia. The last month we have been settled in Ubud, Bali.

When looking at our travel history, each location has been its own chapter in our evolution into finding the right travel and work balance as digital nomads. New Zealand saw us diving into the deep end (without any arm floaties) of the digital nomad swimming pool. We didn't know how SIM cards worked or what a locked American phone meant. We had no clue what a VPN was, so hours were spent figuring out which services would be suitable for us. We spent days in numerous Burger King parking lots using the free WIFI for work and trying to figure out which country to fly to next. Often times we were second-guessing ourselves. "Do we really want to put ourselves through all of these logistical frustrations?"

The SE Asia backpacking leg is about understanding how to build sustainable businesses that allow us to travel and work. We just can't be unpacking and repacking our bags and toggling between APN settings on our mobile router every week if we wish to build a business.

We're finally figuring it out! We feel the need to stay put for at least a month in one spot. This allows us to mitigate the arguments and stress that moving to different countries week-to-week causes. We get more time to focus and explore the location. We get proper rest. We get to know folks in the community – whether it be the locals or the travelers at the coworking spot.

We blog about our adventures at www.nuventuretravels.com.

Did you do the same work before you became a digital

nomad?

Yes. Before we set out traveling, I was already a CPA and Lindsey worked in marketing. We were both working for companies in Colorado Springs, Colorado. After we started traveling, I started my own accounting business, Nuventure CPA (www.nuventurecpa.com), and Lindsey has started freelance work in social media. Also, we have both been developing our writing skills by blogging and writing articles for online publications.

What steps did you take to transition towards becoming a digital nomad? (Or did it just happen naturally?)

We had saved for five years and planned to simply travel the world. We loved the idea of working and traveling, but the reality seemed unreachable. So, we quit our jobs and set out with the mindset to travel, but with the knowledge that there are people working in order to travel longer.

Just before we left on our trip, a buddy asked me to help him file paperwork to start his business. I realized that I could work on his project as we were traveling, so this was the catalyst to changing our mindset that we might be fit to be digital nomads. We then started surrounding ourselves (digitally) with other nomads out there that were already blazing the trail. We realized we needed to find encouragement and tips on how to make this work from those going before us.

The step-by-step process looked a bit like this to us:

1) Googling around and seeing what traveling and working really is and what others are doing.

2) Getting scared and thinking that we couldn't do it.

3) Having friends ask me to do some accounting work. Diving in and learning along the way.

4) Learning and realizing this lifestyle is possible.

5) Trying to grow the business through word of mouth and...

6) Getting excited that it can happen and...

7) Getting scared because holy crap this is my name on this stuff and I feel like I have no idea what I'm doing.

8) Keep traveling aimlessly and realizing that you need more structure to make your business and lifestyle sustainable.

9) Having some really hard emotional conversations with your travel partner and working through the "mud" to find the "white pony".

10) Coming out the other end of the hard crap and realizing that this is going to continue to be hard but it's going to be awesome... because you get to call the shots.

What was your main reason for wanting to live this sort of lifestyle?

FREEDOM! We want the freedom and flexibility to work when

we want and where we want. We want the freedom to be spontaneous, so if we get the invitation to go to Thailand, boom! We can go! If we have the urge to see the Tour de France in person, boom! Let's go!

For the long term, we want freedom to build our family and spend our time the way we see fit. It crushes my heart thinking that I won't be able to go my children's functions because a boss tells me no. I feel that our current working hierarchy might be akin to modern-day indentured servitude.

We have realized that we will probably be building our future family across the country from both of our families. We want to be able to pack up the campervan and head over to Georgia for a month to hang out with our family and not have to ask permission or explain ourselves to anyone.

How do you stay productive?

First, I intentionally wake up early to start the day off well, since I do better work in the mornings. Second, as the day progresses I constantly evaluate my mood and mindset. If I'm tired, then I take a nap because I know that my progress will be less efficient. If I'm stressed then I put everything away, take a break and separate myself from the stressful issue and will come back to it later after I have chilled out.

While working, I utilize the Pomodoro Technique (www.worktravel.co/pomodoro) to keep myself on task. Keeping on task reduces stress and gives me a sense of accomplishment. I use a project management spreadsheet put out by CNQR (www.worktravel.co/cnqr) to keep all the ideas in one spot.

It is important for me to be flexible with what each day brings and have a spontaneous adventure if it comes up. That is what life and travel are all about and that is why I have chosen this lifestyle. So, when I make the decision to go on an adventure, I know there may be consequences of getting the work done later in another block of time.

What does a typical day look like for you?

We wake up around 6.30am. We take care of ourselves in the morning by working out, journaling, and showering. Then, we make sure to have breakfast and coffee together. Around 7.30am or 8am we start working using the Pomodoro Technique. We have lunch and then adventure out or continue working. In the evening we'll do dinner, go out, or stay in. Whatever the day holds.

Those are typical days, but we have days where we get awesome invitations to explore and have spontaneous adventures. This is the point of this lifestyle: having the freedom to make our own decisions!

How do you find new clients for your accountancy business?

As of now, we find new clients through word of mouth and networking when traveling around. It's pretty amazing how natural the marketing is. You meet someone and naturally start talking about what you do. Being that we travel and are building businesses, we naturally describe that process. They get interested and then there is the potential to work together!

What do you wish you'd known at the start?

Hard one. Part of the fun in the journey has been the growth, bit-by-bit, along the way. There have been crazy times of emotional frustration. Just this morning Lindsey had a meltdown because she hasn't figured out a system to prioritize all of the new tasks she has going on. Last week, I went through the same frustration. It was debilitating. I couldn't will myself to be positive and happy. I just napped and sulked around all day. Yes, this episode sounds pitiful and ridiculous, but it is part of the growth process. When you uproot yourself from normalcy and try to build a new lifestyle from scratch, it is going to be tougher than a two-dollar steak. But, that's the beauty of it... personal growth and willing yourself to do the hard things is beautiful.

So, we wish we would have known it would be so emotionally difficult. On the other hand, part of the fun has been working through the hard, emotional times and coming through to the other side.

Our marriage has grown exponentially by sharing in and working through both the sky high and difficult moments together. We see how one another reacts in all kinds of detailed circumstances. When we pay attention, we learn about that and apply the lessons learned going forward.

What's the hardest thing about being a digital nomad?

Ha! Battling the "grass is greener" mentality. No matter what the situation or environment, we always feel if we were experiencing the complete opposite, everything would be better. When we're on the beach, we want to be in the mountains. When we're not working enough, we want to work more. When we feel like we are working too much, we want to work less. We realize we are human and we never seem to be satisfied with the current situation. Self-awareness is the first step! We have to realize our tendencies to cut the bull and just be thankful for where we are. This is a journey it itself!

What tools, equipment or tactics do you rely on for working while travelling?

Hardware:

- Macbook pro

- iPad with bluetooth keyboard

- LG and Motorola phone

- Vodafone mobile wifi hotspot (see **Chapter 4: Be A Productivity Powerhouse** for more information about mobile wifi hotspots)

Credit card churning for hotel and airline points:

- Million Mile Secrets (www.worktravel.co/mms-deals)

- The Points Guy (www.worktravel.co/tpg-deals)

- Award Wallet app (www.worktravel.co/awardwallet)

Meeting "outdoors people" in the location we are traveling:

- Gociety (www.worktravel.co/gociety)

Accommodation, travel-planning and settling in:

- Trusted Housesitters (www.worktravel.co/housesit)

- Carry a backpacking tent, sleeping bags and blow-up pillows

- CamperMate for free campsites in New Zealand (www.worktravel.co/campermate)

- Here Maps (www.worktravel.co/here)

- TripIt (www.worktravel.co/tripit)

- Google Translate (www.worktravel.co/gtranslate)

- Evernote for to-do lists (www.worktravel.co/evernote)

Exercise:

- 7 Minute Workout (www.worktravel.co/seven)

Saving money:

- Sharing meals and limiting alcohol when going out

- Buying and selling instead of renting a campervan in New Zealand

- Mint for budgeting (www.worktravel.co/mint)

Online security

- Purchase a VPN (see **Chapter 3: Guard Your Data** for more on VPNs)

Online storage:

- Google Drive (www.worktravel.co/drive)

- One Drive (www.worktravel.co/onedrive)

- Dropbox (www.worktravel.co/dropbox)

(See **Chapter 7: Run The Best Biz** for more on cloud storage)

Jennifer Harris: Software company owner

Tell us a bit about you and what you do – both in terms of your work and travel habits.

I am a Co-Founder at Inspect Point (www.inspectpoint.com) – a mobile sprinkler inspection software company – that I founded with my boyfriend and two other partners in late 2014.

My boyfriend and I have been living the digital nomad life since 2013 when we took our first trip to SE Asia for three months. Since then, we have decided to take a "slow travel" approach, and avoid having a "home base". Our stays vary based on visas and location, and range from international adventures to US road trips.

Inspect Point is our main focus and plays a huge factor in the cities we visit. Access to reliable internet, time differences, ability to interact with other entrepreneurs, and general interest, all play into how we determine what's next.

What did you do before you became a digital nomad?

Prior to becoming a digital nomad I worked in the marketing department for several technology startups in New York. I was responsible for everything ranging from event management, to email marketing, to lead generation, to campaign creation, to lead management, and more.

What I am currently doing with Inspect Point is very similar to what I did prior to becoming a digital nomad, but because we are a bootstrapped SaaS product, I have been forced to learn many new skills outside my marketing comfort zone, such as basic HTML.

What steps did you take to transition towards becoming a digital nomad?

Becoming a full-time digital nomad took about two years, with a big chunk of my transition spent reading blog posts and books from those already living the digital nomad life – Making It Anywhere, Screw the Nine to Five, Travel Fashion Girl, and Never Ending Voyage, to name a few.

My transition first started with paying down debts while I was still employed full-time. Once debts were paid down, and I was able to quit my job, my focus turned towards getting rid of all of the junk my boyfriend and I had acquired. Some items we were able to sell, some we were able to donate, but most ended up being tossed in one of two (I'm embarrassed to say we needed two) dumpsters. Once we were rid of our junk, we were free to pack our backpacks (which I spent months researching) and jumped aboard a plane for SE Asia.

What was your main reason for wanting to live this sort of lifestyle?

I felt stuck. Stuck in my job. Stuck in my social life. Stuck in everything. Even yoga couldn't cure my angst. I knew I needed to make a change, but wasn't sure what that change was until I read The 4-Hour Work Week (www.worktravel.co/workweek) and started learning more about entrepreneurship.

How do you stay productive?

I use programs such as Trello (www.worktravel.co/trello) and Salesforce (www.worktravel.co/salesforce). With Trello, I love nothing more than moving notes from "Current Sprint", to "Doing", to "Done". With Salesforce, I live by the automated reminders and adore how organized it keeps our team.

[See **Chapter 7: Run The Best Biz** for more about using Trello.]

What does a typical day look like for you?

A typical day involves getting up around 8am, eating breakfast and drinking coffee (I'm addicted), and starting my work day around 9am. I typically take a break around noon to make lunch and go to the gym, and start back to work around 1/1.30pm. Depending upon calls, demos, and time zone, I usually wrap up work around 6pm.

For dinner it depends on the country whether we tend to eat out or cook more. For example, in SE Asia we ate dinner out every night, but in Ireland we did more cooking at our apartment.

After dinner we take a walk around town, grab a drink or an after-dinner coffee, and head back to our apartment. From there we read our Kindles and try to fall asleep by 10pm.

What's the hardest thing about being a digital nomad?

From a work perspective, logistics and timing are the two biggest struggles I currently face, because Inspect Point is an East Coast (US) based business. Time difference and access to internet are huge factors in determining the cities and countries we choose to visit.

From a personal perspective, maintaining relationships with old friends who do not understand my new life and work habits.

What tools, equipment or tactics do you rely on for working while travelling?

Without Skype, Salesforce, Trello, Google, Slack, and Evernote I would be lost. Each plays a key role in how I communicate with leads, customers, and other team members on a daily basis.

- Skype: www.worktravel.co/skype

- Salesforce: www.worktravel.co/salesforce

- Trello: www.worktravel.co/trello

- Slack: www.worktravel.co/slack

- Evernote: www.worktravel.co/evernote

Which countries/cities would you recommend for people who are new to travelling while they work?

I prefer coworking spaces and think they are a great way to meet other travelers passing through and exchange business ideas.

So I'd recommend Ubud in Bali, due to the coworking space there called Hubud (www.worktravel.co/hubud). It's an absolutely amazing coworking space for people new to traveling. They have everything one would need to get work done and meet great people.

How do you make new friends?

Coworking spaces and Meetup.com are both great ways to meet people and make new friends while traveling.

Johanna Read: freelance travel writer and photographer

Tell us a bit about you and what you do – both in terms of your work and travel habits.

I'm a freelance travel writer and photographer. Links to all my articles – and chatty what-I'm-up-to-lately posts – are on my website www.traveleater.net. I'm lucky to write a lot of features on high-end hotels, which I get to stay at for free, as Contributing Editor for an online magazine called Luxury And Boutique Hotels (www.worktravel.co/luxury). I also do occasional management consulting when the issues are interesting and the money is worth taking time away from writing and travelling.

I'm only into my third year of digital nomadism, and so far I've spent about half the time on the road. At the moment I'm home a bit more due to some family commitments (well, "home base" rather than home – I pay family-rate rent at my mum's Vancouver pied-à-terre which mostly sits empty).

I usually go on trips of about two to six months in duration (as a Canadian I would lose my healthcare if I went longer than six months, and a Canadian can't get travel insurance without active provincial health care status; I could go for longer if I sought permission from the government, but I'd like to save calling attention to myself for when I really need it). Last year I got around a fair bit – six continents in less than twelve months.

I was just invited back to China on a press trip (I so love free trips!), which makes my six-continents-in-twelve-months feat quite possible again for this year. Just Australia and South America to get to by April 2016, and South America is in the early planning stages now. If I could find a relatively cheap way of doing it, I might even go to Antarctica!

I'm a mostly solo traveller, though there's a new beau in my life who wants to join me, and luckily his work is amenable to stints of digital nomadism. It will be a bit of an adjustment for me to adapt to non-solo travel though! Especially because when I do the hotel "reviews", I stay two nights at each place – that's a lot of research, meetings, photographing, writing, unpacking, packing and moving around, which is challenging enough as it is. I tend to stay three to four weeks in a city though, to get to know it as much as I can, even though I change where I lay my head so frequently.

Did you do the same work before you became a digital nomad?

Absolutely not. I used to be a policy executive with the Government of Canada. It was an exciting day if I got to go across town for a meeting.

How do you find new clients?

I'm constantly pitching editors, and occasionally PR people, to get writing gigs. I find it bizarre that to be a published writer I only spend about 5% of my time writing; the rest is social media, managing photos, social media, pitching, following-up, social media, and other mind-numbing tasks. And why do social media stats matter so much to editors and PR reps, when one can just purchase them? I explain that I write for other publications with big followings, that posting on my website and social media is just a bonus… sometimes it works, but sometimes they just want to know my stats.

Oh, and I'm also a member of an incredible group of international women writers who are extremely generous in sharing advice and contacts.

What do you do about tax?

I file a Canadian tax return like every other citizen. Luckily (?) I don't make tons of money, so the tax bills aren't horrendous, and I don't think I can be taxed on all my free hotel stays and massages (please don't let me be taxed on those!).

What steps did you take to transition towards becoming a digital nomad? (Or did it just happen naturally?)

I call it my lemons to lemon pie story. I was lucky (yes, lucky) to have a divorce and downsizing happen to me almost at the same time. If either one had happened independently, I would likely have been devastated. But the two together opened my eyes that I could live my retirement dream of travelling and writing at age 43, and not wait until I reached the magic age of 55 having maximized my pension and paid off my mortgage. Life gave me a few lemons, but I made something even better than lemonade – lemon pie.

When my job with the Government of Canada was cut, it literally only took me 20 minutes to stop panicking and realize I could live my retirement dream for real. Ok, it took a few months of figuring out exactly *how* to do that, but 20 minutes to realize I could! With my buy-out package, selling my half of my house to my soon-to-be ex-husband, careful investments, very frugal living and travelling slowly in the developing world, I can afford it too (though the Canadian dollar just hit a decade-plus low of 76 cents U.S., further limiting the countries I can affordably visit …).

What was your main reason for wanting to live this sort of lifestyle?

I realized that if I didn't have a job to go to every day, I didn't need a place to live. And without a place to live, I didn't need a job to pay for it. Travelling almost constantly is the only way I can afford not to have a "real" job.

Oh, and I don't really know how to cook, so I figured if I travel in places with great street food, it might be the only way I won't die of starvation or scurvy.

How do you stay productive?

The Pomodoro Technique (www.worktravel.co/pomodoro) is useful if you're like me and see tangents – useful, but distracting and time-consuming tangents – everywhere. You set an alarm for 25 or 50 minutes, and you're not allowed to do anything except the one specific task you set for yourself until the alarm goes off. Then you get a five or ten minute break. Repeat.

I'm also just entering the stage where I no longer have to do everything that comes my way just to get the byline, the exposure, or even the limited pay. I can pick and choose a little bit to focus on what I find most interesting and useful.

What does a typical day look like for you?

It depends on the day, I have very few typical ones. Lately I've been extremely busy – lots of deadlines, lots of opportunities to pursue, plus I'm doing some management consulting.

If it's a computer day in Vancouver, I aim to be in front of the screen by 9am at the latest, preferably with an iced latte at my right hand. I'll work until I get hungry, and then have breakfast; keep working again until I need another food break around 3:00 and have lunch. I'm a bit of a multitasker so if there's a Netflix show or book I want to catch up on, I feel less guilty if I indulge while I'm eating (I know, that's supposed to be very bad for you). After a bit more computer-time, I'll try (too often unsuccessfully these days) to get outside to run some errands or at least take a walk (which is so gorgeous on the sea-wall, just a block from my Vancouver home base). Often the beau cooks me dinner (isn't that lovely?!). But if I'm by myself, I'll make something fast and not very nutritious and get back to work as quickly as possible. Bed ... I'm a night owl, so it is likely to be about 1am if I'm trying to get to bed early.

If I've been doing management consulting that day, I spend between eight and ten hours at someone's office, and keep an occasional eye on my writing email account for anything urgent. After a quick bite I'll work at home on my writing until I can't focus on the screen any more, at about 11p.m.

And if I'm travelling ... well, every day is different! But I try to balance photographing the hotel I'm writing about, meeting with the manager, and experiencing the hotel (always lovely if the manager hosts me for a meal or in the spa); exploring the city I'm in so I can write about it (and have fun too); taking a few notes to make writing easier when I have time to concentrate; keeping up-to-date on social media (yes with friends but largely for work); and planning for where I'm going next (whether it be organizing more hotels to write about, or figuring out the cheapest but easiest way to get from A to B, or which B I should aim for).

What do you wish you'd known at the start?

That this kind of life was possible. Hell, I wish I'd known that a decade ago!

What's the hardest thing about being a digital nomad?

I find it hard for people to relate to me. Some people don't think I really "work", and then don't understand when I'm not free to join them in an activity, help them do something, or when I complain I'm tired and have too many deadlines. Some people think I lead an extremely cushy life – I'm not saying it isn't cushy; it is! – but they don't realize that I worked my ass off for 25 years to do it, make a lot of sacrifices, and I work more hours in a day than almost everyone I know (and get paid a pittance while they're usually on salary). I don't mind my life in the least – I chose to live this way, and I'd much rather have experiences than money – but it is a bit grating when people don't seem to understand how much effort I have to put in to have it.

And, as a 45-year-old digital nomad, I find there are very few people in my age group doing this. I meet a lot of people in their 20s and 30s who haven't necessarily had a lot of career experience, and a lot of people in their 60s who are in real retirement mode… and that often means our conversations are kind of repetitive. I'm constantly on the look out for salt-and-pepper hair in the hopes of finding someone in their 40s to talk to!

What tools, equipment or tactics do you rely on for working while travelling?

I travel with just my camera, iPhone and my iPad – the added convenience of the laptop doesn't justify the weight.

I try to jot notes down in the Notes app whenever an idea strikes, but that means I have too many notes that get backed up too frequently on both devices, so I don't trust which version is the most complete and I don't have time to check and delete the old ones… they're getting close to unusable. I need to clean them up and get a better system.

Part 2: Families who travel

The Hiller family _ 312

The Suter family _ 319

The Langford family _ 325

The Hiller family

Kalli Hiller is married to Jacob, and they have a son called Ryder.

Tell us a bit about you and your family!

Jacob and I met in college, got married and shortly thereafter moved to Germany. We didn't intentionally choose this lifestyle- it kind of chose us as our online businesses grew and our list of places we'd like to see did too. We have a jump training program for athletes, an ebook software company, and a customer relationship management system for network marketers, all completely managed online. We have an outsourcing team based out of the Philippines. We also have a real estate agent in Florida who we partner with to flip houses and buy rentals. Our son is three years old. He has been to 35 countries and we have been to 55 +. We currently have no home base.

Our websites are www.jumpmanual.com, www.myebookmaster.com, and www.portableprofessionals.com.

Did you have Ryder before you became digital nomads, or vice versa?

Ryder was born in Mexico. At that point we had been travelling full time for three years.

What are the logistical issues to be aware of?

Not really sure what logistics? Kids are easier to travel with than pets.

How do you plan travel days?

I spend some time looking for the cheapest flight. Lately I've been into using Secretflying.com and Flight Daily Deals newsletter to find them but I also use Momondo (www.worktravel.co/momondo) and Skyscanner (www.worktravel.co/skyscanner). Then we use information websites like Lonely Planet (www.worktravel.co/planet) and Wikitravel (www.worktravel.co/wikitravel) to ensure the best way to get to our hotel usually by public transportation. We put our hotel into Google Maps (www.worktravel.co/gmaps) in advance of traveling so we can find our hotel even if we don't have internet.

Which means of transport do you prefer, and why?

Personally I prefer train, you can have as much baggage as you want, there's no TSA, and you can see the countryside. I really don't care for flying but it's become more necessary with a child because 20 hours in a train sometimes just isn't feasible with a little kid who needs to run around.

How do you manage childcare?

We occasionally find babysitters through hotels or through church. In places like Bali and the Philippines childcare is so cheap – something like $1 per hour – that Ryder had a full time nanny. I also like finding playplaces with free wifi which is increasingly common these days.

How is schooling/education arranged? (Or how will it be arranged when Ryder is older?)

It will depend on where we are living at the time. I would like to put him in a local school if possible.

What about *stuff*? Kids seem to need a lot of it! Do you take it with you or buy it when you arrive?

Ryder doesn't need that much stuff. I think Jacob and I tend to accumulate much more than he does! We bring most of it with us. Clothes and toys. Then as things get misplaced along the way, as they are wont to do when moving so often, we replace them where we're at. As a baby Ryder needed more – a baby bed, portable potty, and portable high chair are all things we've left behind as he's grown older.

Is it difficult not having a support system? Or do you create one in the places that you travel to?

Yes. And yes. Having a child makes it easier in some ways to create a support system because children make friends quickly and it's easy to just go to where kids congregate. Play groups, libraries, kids museums, and playgrounds are all places to make connections. It's definitely a top priority to reach out to people and ask them to dinner or events with us. Even a one time connection is valuable to the full-time nomad.

How does Ryder keep in touch/develop relationships with relatives like grandparents, uncles and aunts?

Ryder gets the concept of Skype. He just gets it. His grandparents have toys at their house and they play with toys over the screen. We look at pictures of them together and we talk about them a lot. It's important to me that he has a relationship with them. They come to us and we visit them a couple times a year. It's really not so different to living in a different state like a majority of other Americans do.

What does Ryder think of this lifestyle?

Ryder's never known anything else, but he loves traveling. I'm not being biased here. He's a typical boy – he loves planes, trains, boats and cars, and fortunately, he also loves museums and trying all types of foods.

How does/will Ryder make friends and maintain friendships?

Ryder has a couple of "make friends" tricks. One is to start running in an attempt to get the other child to chase him. Another is to copy exactly what they are saying and doing until a friendship is born. Both tactics work very well. Kids are funny. Ryder has already had a couple of best friends that he still talks about as well as cousins that, though only spending a relatively brief amount of time, really made a deep impression.

There's a saying that "The best thing parents can do for their children is to give them roots and wings." How do you ensure that you give Ryder "roots" as well as "wings"?

A source of confidence for children, studies show, is knowing where they come from – family history and stories. We talk a lot about what we value in both Jacob's and my families, and we've visited both Scotland and Germany for family history reasons. We have dinner together every night, and we try to remember to emphasize that we prioritize relationships and friendships over anything else. We also have *something* of a routine, though it's not exact, including bedtime rituals.

What are some good cities/countries in which to be a digital nomad family?

Jacob and I have had varying experiences. But we both loved:

Japan, Austria, Guatemala, Mexico, New Zealand, and Vanuatu.

Any bad ones?

It depends on what you're looking for. I don't think I could stay in Estonia too long – it's too cold both weather-wise and interpersonally for me. But it's actually a digital destination – it has some of the fastest internet in the world, and internet-friendly business laws. I think every destination is worthy in its own right.

How do you find accommodation?

Booking.com (www.worktravel.co/booking), Airbnb (www.worktravel.co/airbnb), VRBO (www.worktravel.co/vrbo), FlipKey (www.worktravel.co/flipkey) and 9flats (www.worktravel.co/9flats) are all ones we've used. Sometimes we will use a rental company specific to the location, like Sakura House in Japan (www.worktravel.co/sakura). What we're looking for is the most inexpensive place we can get downtown. We like to be in the heart of the city.

Do you have any specific requirements when it comes to accommodation?

Ideally, Jacob likes to have a home office. I've almost never had a dishwasher or an oven, but after our last stay with both, I'm feeling like I'm going to have to look for those here on out. It was so nice.

Even if it's worth it… do you think this lifestyle is harder than if you were to stay in one place with Ryder (like regular people do!)?

I really don't know. I've never known anything else with a child.

It can be lonely when we first arrive to a new destination, and it's sometimes frustrating to not have a full kitchen and deal with language barriers and other cultural differences, but I also think staying at home and having an American suburban lifestyle would be its own challenge. I do know that I love our lifestyle, I love being a mom, and Ryder is happy, so I wouldn't change a thing! I also think as he gets older we will become more stationary. Multiple kids would complicate, but not halt, this lifestyle – we've met enough large traveling families by this point to know that by now!

Anything else you'd like to mention?

Traveling with a child has only enriched our lifestyle. We feel very fortunate.

The Suter family

Allison Suter is married to Jonathan, and they have a daughter called Clara.

Tell us a bit about you and your family!

We started SimpleTax (www.simpletax.ca) – a pay-what-you-want Canadian tax filing software product – in 2012. Before that, we had more traditional careers (I was a lawyer and Jonathan worked in tech). We have a home base in Vancouver, and we try to do at least one long (2.5+ month) and several one-month trips a year.

We have one 17-month-old daughter. Our last big adventure

was when she was 15 months old.

We're a bit different than a typical digital nomad family as we have a home base that we try to stay in 6+ months a year (because Vancouver is awesome).

Did you have Clara before you became digital nomads, or vice versa?

We had Clara after we'd been digital nomading for just over two years.

How do you plan travel days?

This has been evolving. When she was very little (2-6 months) we didn't have (or need much of) a strategy: snuggles and nursing can get you through almost anything. Even up to about the age of one, she was a great napper in her baby carrier, which got us through most situations. Now that Clara is a young toddler, if it's a short flight we try to get it done before midday (naptime) as she's much more patient in the morning. This also means she can sleep while we get things packed up to go. For long flights, we try for after dinner (around bedtime); that has been hit or miss so far.

If you have a child who is lap-infant age but you can afford an extra seat for long flights, we highly recommend it. Having her in her carseat on our longest flights has been so helpful.

We pack a bunch of little (quiet) toys and many, many snacks (cheese is a favourite). All bets are off on travel days, if she wants to watch TV for three hours on a plane or have two extra cups of milk, that is a-ok with us.

Which means of transport do you prefer, and why?

Because we are in Canada, we pretty much only fly anywhere!

How do you manage childcare?

During our last trip, Clara was still taking two naps a day so we both worked during naps and split work hours for the rest of the days (six days a week). We also try to arrange trips near grandma and grandpa, which has been helpful (once you work out a formal schedule). As she gets older we'll look into local daycares and nannies by tapping into expat message boards and Facebook groups!

What about *stuff*? Kids seem to need a lot of it! Do you take it with you or buy it when you arrive?

While we are firmly out of the realm of carry-on only, I find that we still are able to travel lightly! We bring a baby carrier, Clara's travel cot (Phil&Teds), a travel high chair (Phil&Teds), a "hybrid" stroller (Babyhome Emotion), and a light carseat (Cosco Scenera). Each of these items is specifically designed to be light and portable. We can easily get those items, a large suitcase, a large backpack, and a small backpack and a diaper bag onto a commuter train. For everything else (food, diapers, etc.) we bring enough for the travel day plus four days and then buy a proper supply on arrival. We've become very flexible about brands!

- Phil&Teds on Amazon: www.worktravel.co/philteds
- Babyhome Emotion stroller: www.worktravel.co/babyhome
- Cosco Scenera carseat: www.worktravel.co/carseat (US only)

Is it difficult not having a support system? Or do you create one in the places that you travel to?

It's becoming more difficult as Clara gets older – she was a very relaxed baby (we were lucky)!

How does Clara keep in touch/develop relationships with relatives like grandparents, uncles and aunts?

Two ways:

1. Plan destinations to be near/with them (we spent ten weeks near or with my parents in the first year after Clara was born).

2. FaceTime and Skype are extremely effective!

What does Clara think of this lifestyle?

TBD! We think it makes her more adaptable.

What are some good cities/countries in which to be a digital nomad family?

We loved Madrid and Sitges in Spain (good amenities and very family-friendly cities). Spain had the best generic diapers of any country we've travelled to!

How do you find accommodation?

Mostly Airbnb (or the local equivalent if Airbnb doesn't have a strong foothold).

Do you have any specific requirements when it comes to accommodation?

A small space for the baby cot (preferably a small second bedroom/office, but we can be flexible). A small office nook or space is helpful (so that someone can always get work done in a sane environment if possible). A washing machine is critical. We pour over pictures of the apartment trying to determine if the space is baby-safe (e.g., too many trinkets, bookshelves, ledges, stairways, windows, etc.). If it's up several flights of stairs, a lift or a place to stash the stroller in the lobby is important.

Even if it's worth it… do you think this lifestyle is harder than if you were to stay in one place with your children (like regular people do!)?

So far, it really depends on the space. If we are in a great space I think it's actually easier (at least on us). We find that we have less to "do" when we aren't at our home base. When you arrive in a new city you have no friends, no family, less cleaning, and less general maintenance – and because of that we get to spend more time having family adventures.

If we are in a not-so-good space, it's much, much harder than staying in one place.

This could change as Clara gets older/our family grows. My brother-in-law (who has older children) decided to stay put somewhere once his eldest started school.

The Langford family

Ryan Langford is married to Steph, and they have FIVE children under the age of ten! Abbie, Caden, Johanna, Kepler and Oliver. Together they run a number of businesses as they travel the world:

- Resound School of Music (www.resoundschool.com): a local music school which employs over 20 teachers and two full-time office staff.

- Keeper of the Home (www.keeperofthehome.org): a natural living blog, which Steph runs with the help of a fabulous group of contributing writers and admin team.

- Ultimate Bundles (www.ultimate-bundles.com): seasonal bundles of digital products (like ebooks and courses) sold at no-brainer prices.

- EntreFamily (www.entrefamily.com): a blog about their journey as digital nomads.

Did you have children before you became digital nomads, or vice versa?

We had done a bunch of travelling abroad before we had kids, but didn't really have the freedom to travel the way that we wanted to until we had four of them!

What are the logistical issues to be aware of?

Surprisingly, the logistics are not as hard as you might imagine. Of course, you need to make sure that you don't lose anybody (that's a biggie!), but housing and transportation is largely the same (if not a little bit bigger) than if we were travelling without kids.

How do you plan travel days?

Usually we plan our travel around work events/meetings, but we'll also adjust our dates for cheaper transportation costs. With seven of us, saving $100 on a flight adds up quickly.

Which means of transport do you prefer, and why?

When we first started travelling with our kids, we swore we'd never rent a car, but that has become our favourite mode of transportation because of the flexibility it affords us. We love being able to explore places on a whim, and not have to wait on train/bus schedules, etc.

How do you manage childcare?

We don't tend to get as much one-on-one time with each other as we'd like to, although we've learned to adapt. Instead of going out for dinner, one of us might go pick something up, and then we'll eat together just outside of the house, on a balcony, etc.

We have been blessed, though, to meet up with friends from time to time, and "trade" babysitting with each other. We recently spent a month with friends in France, and we traded babysitting at least once a week. It was wonderful and is one of the big perks of travelling with friends.

How is schooling/education arranged?

We tend to travel in two modes:

1. "Tourist/Vacation" Mode, where we go hard for two to three weeks and see and experience everything that we can see in a certain place.

2. "Living Abroad" Mode, where we find a place to settle, and

have a semi-normal life and routine.

When we're in "Tourist/Vacation" Mode, we're really slack with our kids' schoolwork. We feel that the experiences they are having are far more valuable then what they could be learning through the curriculum. The extent of their formal education at this point is reading on their Kindles (for the older kids), and drawing (for everybody), and some education games on our iPad as an occasional treat.

When we're in "Living Abroad" Mode, we typically spend four days per week at home in a regular routine that includes schoolwork for the kids as well as time for Steph and I to work on our businesses. If we've been in "Tourist/Vacation" Mode for a while, we may buckle down a little bit more during this time to catch up some things if we've fallen behind, although we don't stress about it too much.

What about *stuff*? Kids seem to need a lot of it! Do you take it with you or buy it when you arrive?

Honestly, kids really *don't* need that much stuff. Each of our kids carry their own backpack, and have 2-3 toys, plus a notebook and paper to draw with. They quickly learned to be creative and the world become their entertainment. Sticks, rocks, dirt, walls, structures, people – you name it – have all proven to be superior to any toy made in China.

How do your children make friends and maintain friendships?

This, of course, is one of the hardest things for not just the kids, but the whole family. We definitely make an effort to connect the kids with their friends at home (and abroad) through Skype and FaceTime. This is easier when we're settled somewhere for a longer period of time.

But we also encourage our kids to make friends wherever we go. We seek out opportunities to connect with both locals and expats to give them (and ourselves) that opportunity. Many of our kids' favourite memories from our trips are related to someone they met while we were travelling. Sometimes we make those connections through a friend-of-a-friend-of-a-friend, sometimes by finding a church to attend, and sometimes just by making the effort to connect with someone we just met. All in all, everybody has developed some great relationships through our travels.

Resources: List of links

Here's a big ol' list of all the links used throughout the book. You can also find them at www.worktravel.co/links.

CHAPTER 1: SETTLE IN FAST

Maps, directions and notekeeping

Google Keep (note-taking app): www.worktravel.co/keep

Google Maps: www.worktravel.co/gmaps

Google Maps – how to store destinations as favourites: www.worktravel.co/mapfaves

Google Maps Directions: www.worktravel.co/directions

Google Maps list of offline maps: www.worktravel.co/offlinemaps

Google Maps - how to download an offline map: www.worktravel.co/offlinemaps2

OsmAnd (offline maps with navigation): www.worktravel.co/

osmand

Here Maps (offline maps): www.worktravel.co//here

Taxis

Uber (taxi app): www.worktravel.co/uber

Uber (list of cities): www.worktravel.co/ubercities

MyTaxi (taxi app): www.worktravel.co/mytaxi

Lyft (taxi app): www.worktravel.co/lyft

Gett (taxi app): www.worktravel.co/gett

Languages/translation

Google Translate: www.worktravel.co/gtranslate

XE (currency conversion): www.worktravel.co/xe

Anki (flashcard app): www.worktravel.co/anki

Duolingo (language learning): www.worktravel.co/duolingo

Michel Thomas (language learning): www.worktravel.co/michel

Money/cost of living

Numbeo (cost of living in different cities): www.worktravel.co/

numbeo

GlobeTipping (global tipping app for iPhone): www.worktravel.co/globetipping

Global Tip Calculator Pro (global tipping app for Android): www.worktravel.co/globalpro

SIM cards

Prepaid with Data (info on SIM cards around the world): www.worktravel.co/prepaid

TripAdvisor forum (search for info on "monthly prepaid SIM 3G": www.worktravel.co/taforum

Lonely Planet forum (has useful Q&As about SIMs around the world): www.worktravel.co/planetforum

Restaurant, cafe, attraction, etc. reviews and info

Foursquare (good for Europe): www.worktravel.co/foursquare

Yelp (good for US and Europe): www.worktravel.co/yelp

Spotted by Locals: www.worktravel.co/spotted

Tabelog (Japan): www.worktravel.co/tabelog

Vayable (marketplace where locals offer unique tours): www.worktravel.co/vayable

Receive mail

Poste Restante (Wikipedia page): www.worktravel.co/post

Amazon Lockers: www.worktravel.co/locker

DHL Packstations (pickup lockers in Germany): www.worktravel.co/packstation

Doddle (pickup lockers in the UK): www.worktravel.co/doddle

My Pick Box (pickup lockers in Spain): www.worktravel.co/pickup

Parcel (get all mail delivered to a unique address, which they'll then deliver at a convenient time): www.worktravel.co/parcel

Mail-forwarding services

UK Postbox: www.worktravel.co/ukpost

Earth Class Mail (USA): www.worktravel.co/earthclass

ClevverMail (Germany): www.worktravel.co/clevver

Aussie Mail Man: www.worktravel.co/aussie

Find/make friends

Find A Nomad: www.worktravel.co/findanomad

Create Your Nomadtopia: www.worktravel.co/topia

ShareDesk (coworking spaces): www.worktravel.co/sharedesk

Fitness

Walking/cycling/running:

OsmAnd (offline maps): www.worktravel.co/osmand

Ride With GPS (routes): www.worktravel.co/gps

Lanyard (for holding phone and following route while running/cycling): www.worktravel.co/lanyard

Apartment-friendly exercise videos:

Fitness Blender: www.worktravel.co/blender

DDP Yoga: www.worktravel.co/ddp

Do You Yoga: www.worktravel.co/yoga

Focus T25: www.worktravel.co/t25

Sleek Technique: www.worktravel.co/sleek

Community fitness:

Project Awesome (London): www.worktravel.co/awesome

November Project (USA): www.worktravel.co/november

CHAPTER 2: GET TO GRIPS WITH MONEY AND TAXES

Credit/debit card charges

If you're from the UK...

Comparison of debit card fees: www.worktravel.co/ukdebit

Comparison of credit card fees: www.worktravel.co/ukcredit

Best specialist travel credit cards: www.worktravel.co/uktravelcredit

Info about travel debit cards: www.worktravel.co/uktraveldebit

Supercard (still in testing phase at the time of writing, and only currently available for UK residents): www.worktravel.co/supercard

Number26 (still in testing phase at the time of writing, and also available throughout the rest of Europe): www.worktravel.co/26

If you're from the US...

List of credit cards that don't charge a foreign transaction fee: www.worktravel.co/ustravelcredit

List of banks and their debit card transaction/ATM fees: www.worktravel.co/ustraveldebit

Info about avoiding credit/debit card transaction fees: www.worktravel.co/avoidfees

Charles Schwab (reimburses ATM fees): www.worktravel.co/schwab

If you're from Australia...

Info on credit/debit cards and fees: www.worktravel.co/finder

More info in the book if you're from anywhere else!

Calculate your cost of living

The Birdy: www.worktravel.co/birdy

Numbeo's cost-of-living tool: www.worktravel.co/numbeo

Trail Wallet: www.worktravel.co/trailwallet

Taxes

Greenback Expat Tax Services: www.worktravel.co/greenback

Small Business Bodyguard: www.worktravel.co/bodyguard

Flag Theory: www.worktravel.co/flag

Foreign Earned Income Exclusion (US residents only): www.worktravel.co/irs

CHAPER 3: GUARD YOUR DATA

Protect Your Tech (book): www.worktravel.co/protectyourtech

HTTP Everywhere: www.worktravel.co/httpseverywhere

Torguard VPN: www.worktravel.co/torguard

LastPass (password management): www.worktravel.co/lastpass

CHAPTER 4: BE A PRODUCTIVITY POWERHOUSE

Have a routine

The Tiny Habits Method (website and free course): www.worktravel.co/tinyhabits

Coach Me (app that helps you reach your goals): www.worktravel.co/coach

Mini Habits: Smaller Habits, Bigger Results (book by Stephen Guise): www.worktravel.co/minihabits

The Checklist Manifesto: How to Get Things Right (book by Atul Gawande): www.worktravel.co/checklist

Quora Q&A – "What are the best daily routines of highly productive people?": www.worktravel.co/quora

Quora Q&A – "What are the best ways for non 9-5 types to build structure and social interaction into their daily routines?": www.worktravel.co/quora2

Stay focused and filter out distractions

Unroll Me (unsubscribe from emails): www.worktravel.co/

unroll

Gmail "plus sign" trick: www.worktravel.co/plustrick

Trello: www.worktravel.co/trello

Pomodoro Technique: www.worktravel.co/pomodoro

Pomodoto (Pomodoro timer): www.worktravel.co/pomodoto

You Can Book Me (appointment-booking software): www.worktravel.co/bookme

iDoneThis (track what you've achieved): www.worktravel.co/donethis

AskMeEvery (track what you've achieved): www.worktravel.co/askme

Kransen headphones: www.worktravel.co/kransen

ShareDesk (coworking spaces): www.worktravel.co/sharedesk

Coffitivity (concentration app): www.worktravel.co/coffitivity

Focus@Will (concentration app): www.worktravel.co/focus

Optimise your workspace

Roost laptop stand: www.worktravel.co/roost

Portable keyboards: www.worktravel.co/keyboard

Mini-mouse: www.worktravel.co/mouse

ZestDesk (standing desk): www.worktravel.co/zestdesk

StandStand (standing desk): www.worktravel.co/standstand

Kinivo ZX100 laptop speakers: www.worktravel.co/zx100

Deal with wifi issues

Wifi speed test: www.worktravel.co/speedtest

Huawei E5330 mobile hotspot: www.worktravel.co/hotspot

Didlogic (cheap international calls without internet): www.worktravel.co/didlogic

Skype To Go: www.worktravel.co/skypetogo

Google Docs Offline: www.worktravel.co/docsoffline

CHAPTER 5: FREELANCE FROM ANYWHERE

Emailing

Boomerang (to delay when an email gets sent): www.worktravel.co/boomerang

Scheduling

World Time Buddy: www.worktravel.co/worldtimebuddy

Doodle: www.worktravel.co/doodle

Mixmax: www.worktravel.co/mixmax

You Can Book Me: www.worktravel.co/bookme

Phone/video calls

Buy a Skype Number: www.worktravel.co/skypenumber

Zoom (alternative to Skype): www.worktravel.co/zoom

GoToMeeting (alternative to Skype): www.worktravel.co/gotomeeting

Join Me (alternative to Skype): www.worktravel.co/joinme

Didlogic (cheap international calls without internet): www.worktravel.co/didlogic

Skype To Go: www.worktravel.co/skypetogo

Screen sharing

Screenleap: www.worktravel.co/screenleap

Document signing

HelloSign: www.worktravel.co/hellosign

EchoSign: www.worktravel.co/echosign

Getting paid

PayPal: www.worktravel.co/paypal

Stripe: www.worktravel.co/stripe

Freshbooks (for information about PayPal Business Payments): www.worktravel.co/freshbooks

Harvest (for information about PayPal Business Payments): www.worktravel.co/harvest

TransferWise (cross-currency payments): www.worktravel.co/transferwise

CHAPTER 6: HIRE LIKE A CHAMP

Hire remote contractors

Upwork (formerly Elance/oDesk): www.worktravel.co/upwork

Guru: www.worktravel.co/guru

Freelancer: www.worktravel.co/freelancer

Gigster: www.worktravel.co/gigster

99 Designs: www.worktravel.co/99designs

Crowdspring: www.worktravel.co/crowdspring

Fancy Hands: www.worktravel.co/fancyhands

Information about "milestones": www.worktravel.co/milestones

Screencast-o-matic (record screencasts): www.worktravel.co/screencast

Hire permanent employees

Working Mums (UK): www.worktravel.co/workingmums

Hire My Mom (US): www.worktravel.co/hiremymom

Remotive: www.worktravel.co/remotive

Remote OK: www.worktravel.co/remoteok

WFH.io: www.worktravel.co/wfh

We Work Remotely: www.worktravel.co/wework

Authentic Jobs: www.worktravel.co/authentic

Upwork: www.worktravel.co/upwork

Information about KPIs: www.worktravel.co/kpi

Topgrading (hiring tips and resources): www.worktravel.co/topgrading

Buffer's 45-day contract period: www.worktravel.co/bootcamp

CHAPTER 7: RUN THE BEST BIZ

Team chat software

Slack: www.worktravel.co/slack

HipChat: www.worktravel.co/hipchat

Structured meetings and ad-hoc calls

Mastering The Rockefeller Habits (book): www.worktravel.co/rockefeller

World Time Buddy: www.worktravel.co/worldtimebuddy

Google Calendar: www.worktravel.co/calendar

Zoom (alternative to Skype): www.worktravel.co/zoom

Appear.in (alternative to Skype): www.worktravel.co/appear

Screen sharing

Screenleap: www.worktravel.co/screenleap

Giving tutorials and training

Screencast-o-matic: www.worktravel.co/screencast

ScreenFlow (Mac): www.worktravel.co/screenflow

Camtasia (Windows): www.worktravel.co/camtasia

Procedures

Google Drive: www.worktravel.co/drive

Process Street: www.worktravel.co/process

Project management

Trello: www.worktravel.co/trello

Basecamp: www.worktravel.co/basecamp

Asana: www.worktravel.co/asana

Teamwork: www.worktravel.co/teamwork

Wikipedia's "Comparison of project management software" page: www.worktravel.co/pmtools

Cloud storage

Dropbox: www.worktravel.co/dropbox

OneDrive: www.worktravel.co/onedrive

Google Drive: www.worktravel.co/drive

Information on Google Drive "offline mode": www.worktravel.co/docsoffline

Box: www.worktravel.co/box

Amazon Cloud Drive: www.worktravel.co/acd

Other useful tools and resources

LastPass (password management): www.worktravel.co/lastpass

HelloSign (document signing): www.worktravel.co/hellosign

EchoSign (document signing): www.worktravel.co/echosign

Sqwiggle (video team chat): www.worktravel.co/sqwiggle

Zapier (task automation): www.worktravel.co/zapier

IFTTT (task automation): www.worktravel.co/ifttt

Also by the author…

Protect Your Tech:

Your geek-free guide to a secure and private digital life

If your password for every website is "monkey" or "iloveyou"… you need to read this book.

Learn, in one afternoon, everything you need to know to keep your personal data secure and private when you work, shop and play online – using (mostly) free online tools.

Protect Your Tech is an entertaining, action-oriented guide to safeguarding your digital life. With simple, jargon-free explanations, you'll learn easy steps you can take to keep your personal data safely under wraps.

Buy it on Amazon: www.worktravel.co/protectyourtech.

Find out:

- How easy it is for someone to crack your online

passwords – even "clever" ones like "Pa55w0rd!"

- The simple, but crucial steps you need to take to protect yourself when you're using your phone or laptop from a cafe, airport or other public place.

- How to make sure that even if your device gets stolen, the thief can't find out anything about you.

- The dangers you're exposed to if you use a "cloud" storage solution like Dropbox or Google Drive – and what to do about it.

- How to avoid getting scammed when you're buying online.

- Much more!

Contains step-by-step instructions for desktop (Windows and Mac) and mobile (iOS and Android) devices.

Buy it on Amazon: www.worktravel.co/protectyourtech.

Also by the author...

Travel Like A Pro:

Road-Tested Tips for Digital Nomads and Frequent Travelers

A fun, info-packed read to turn your travel from "panicked" to "pro"

It's an amazing privilege to be able to zip all over the planet. But the process of travel can be exhausting, panic-inducing and complicated – even when you do it all the time.

Perplexing flight options, overpriced accommodation and dragging a wobbly-wheeled suitcase through an awful airport are enough to take the gloss off even the funnest of trips.

It doesn't have to be that way: **Travel Like A Pro** is an entertaining, practical guide to becoming effortlessly mobile. With road-tested tips on everything from packing and flights to visas and insurance – and countless links to extra recommendations and resources – it's for anyone who wants to skip the stress and glide through their globetrotting life.

Buy it on Amazon: www.worktravel.co/protravel.

In this book you'll learn:

- What you should always take with you, and what's really not worth the extra weight

- How to protect yourself with the right insurance

- A system for booking the cheapest flights – without being forced into indirect routes and layovers, or having the experience take over your life

- Handy hints for surviving the airport and hacking carry-on baggage allowances

- Where to find the best travel gear

- Which handy websites will make your trips a triumph

This book isn't about "seeing the world on $50 a day". It's for people who want to get there and get sorted – minus the aggravation and confusion that plague most people who just take a couple of trips a year.

With practical advice, plenty of jokes and *over a hundred links to extra resources and material*, **Travel Like A Pro** is the perfect travel companion for digital nomads, frequent travellers and anyone who wants to see the world but get the hell on with it.

Buy it on Amazon: www.worktravel.co/protravel.

Thank yous

Christopher Sutton, Jewels Velky, Pete Domican, Kelly O'Laughlin, Shayna Oliveira, Michael Anderson, Lewis Smith and Louise Rees: you rock. THANK YOU for reading through and commenting on a book that's about triple the size I told you it would be. Your advice, insights and "Is that even a Britishism or is it just a Mishism??" comments have helped make this book a shit ton better than I could ever manage by myself.

Julian Barton, Skylr Monaghan, Simon Truran, Katarzyna Majchrzycka, Maurizio Barone, Katharina Krāwinkel, Ruth Vahle, Kara Byun, Tara Spencer, Floss Slade (mum), Sue Sames, Sam Floy, Ricardo Aitken, Adam Nubern and Lindsey Nubern: you were so generous with your ideas, perspectives and encouragement on specific chapters of the book – thank you.

Mark Gibson, Carolyn Kopprasch, Crystal Bryant, Jennifer Harris, Andres Zuleta, Adam Nubern, Kathryn O'Halloran, Eli Trier, Allison Suter, Ryan Langford, Kalli Hiller, Lewis Smith, Jewels Velky, Blake Boles, Johanna Read and Pete Domican: the tips and experiences you share in your interviews will be invaluable to anyone who's planning to live this lifestyle.

And Robbie D: well, you're sitting right next to me. So I'll just thank you in person.

About the author

Mish Slade has spent three years as a digital nomad – running her businesses from 20 different countries with her husband, and blogging about the experience on www.makingitanywhere.com.

She has travel down to the finest of arts, yet still can't *quite* be trusted not to make jokes while going through security.

Printed in Poland
by Amazon Fulfillment
Poland Sp. z o.o., Wrocław